Future-Ready Now

Neuroscience-based Career
and Life Design

Dr. Sweta Adatia MD

Future-Ready Now
Copyright © 2022 Dr. Sweta Adatia MD
First published in 2022

Print: 978-1-76124-070-6
E-book: 978-1-76124-071-3
Hardback: 978-1-76124-072-0

All rights reserved. No part of this book may be reproduced, stored in a retrieval system, or transmitted by any means (electronic, mechanical, photocopying, recording, or otherwise) without written permission from the author.

Because of the dynamic nature of the Internet, any web addresses or links contained in this book may have changed since publication and may no longer be valid. The information in this book is based on the author's experiences and opinions. The views expressed in this book are solely those of the author and do not necessarily reflect the views of the publisher; the publisher hereby disclaims any responsibility for them.

The author of this book does not dispense any form of medical, legal, financial, or technical advice either directly or indirectly. The intent of the author is solely to provide information of a general nature to help you in your quest for personal development and growth. In the event you use any of the information in this book, the author and the publisher assume no responsibility for your actions. If any form of expert assistance is required, the services of a competent professional should be sought.

Publishing information
Publishing and design facilitated by Passionpreneur Publishing
A division of Passionpreneur Organization Pty Ltd
ABN: 48640637529

Melbourne, VIC | Australia
www.passionpreneurpublishing.com

This book is dedicated to all **humane** *beings.*
The human being is endowed but being human is incredible.

"This book contributes in an extraordinary way to the concept of 'future-ready'. It is a superb addition to the art and science of career discovery and career choices—Dr Adatia's approach is fresh, different and prepares students for a world that will keep on changing radically. It is certainly one of the most meaningful publications in this field in the 21st century."

—Dr Kobus Neethling
Creator of the NBI Whole-Brain Instruments,
Guinness World Record holder, and author of
a number of international publications and TV series.

Table of Contents

Acknowledgements		vii
Introduction		ix
Chapter 1	Arranged-Cum-Love Career: What a Dilemma!	1
Chapter 2	What's all the Fuss About Career Discovery?	19
Chapter 3	The Who, What, When, Where and How of Generation Alpha	37
Chapter 4	The World of Work in the 21st Century: Expect the Unexpected	55
Chapter 5	Is There a Perfect Career Tool?	75
Chapter 6	What *is* the Difference in the Difference?	93
Chapter 7	*Mybraindesign*®: The Secret Source to 'Know Thyself'	109
Chapter 8	The End Point for Your Career Choice is the New Beginning for Your Life	143
Chapter 9	Let's Live By Purpose, and Not By Accident	159
Chapter 10	Flow and Grow: Stretching the Thinking through New Hobbies and Activities	171
Chapter 11	Adult Bonus Chapter	183
Conclusion		203

About the Author	207
Extras	209
Want More Resources?	223
About the Book	227
Testimonials	229

Acknowledgements

'Acknowledging the good that you already have in your life is the foundation for all the abundance.'

— EKHART TOLLE

To my spiritual teacher Swamini Vimalananda, a monk for being the best critic and allowing me to grow *wisely* and *widely*.

To my dearest parents Smita Adatia and Dr. Prakash Adatia who allowed me to *be* me.

To my dearest friends – Dr. Preeti Sahota, Dr. Dhanashri Chonkar, and Rudra Dasgupta. With a special shout-out to Indrani Dasgupta, manager *par excellence* (both in life and work) who made me realise the dark sides of my personality and helped me patiently work on it. Heated gold becomes an ornament. Thank you for showing up in this lifetime.

To my chief colleagues Dr. Raza Siddique, CEO of the Arabian Healthcare Group, and Dr. Marc Gauer, CEO of RAK Hospital. Their mere presence is inspiring.

To all my other colleagues and researchers for this book along with my dearest patients, I give my thanks, especially for your never-ending blessings.

I want to *be* more and *do* more. The journey has just begun.

Introduction

What if we could prepare the children and young people in our lives for successful careers and rewarding lives long before the end of their high school education? What if that choice could be built on understanding their unique way of thinking and being in this world, rather than the pressure of having to choose a job to suit their options when they finish college? What if we could 'future-ready' them much earlier, and in doing so, empower them to design life, not just a career?

I have one of the best jobs in the world – I work to help people across the globe (my childhood dream). I help my patients embrace a healthy life and I help to release students/adults stuck in their career choices. I did not land accidentally in this job. I had to endure a roller-coaster ride before I could reach this stage of my life.

I could not have been happier or more fulfilled (accomplished too, I hold a doctorate in neuroscience) if I was merely a 'brain plumber', that is, a neurologist. I often joke in my seminars and say it is very easy to fix a broken brain but difficult to kindle a normal brain. My kick in the morning, waking up each day, is how I help students and adults stuck in their career choices. The happy chemicals – dopamine and serotonin – gush through my brain when I see the joyful and relieved faces of parents and students.

While in my career practice, I can help a few thousand in my lifetime, through building a process that is embraced globally, I can reach a few million. This legacy in career life choices is my endeavour.

My own career journey, from medicine to neurology and an MBA from Cambridge University (one of the top five highest QS ranking universities in the world), forms the catalyst for this book. Curiosity to know myself, or my thinking self, became the force behind the development of *Mybraindesign*® – a tool showcasing how you think and how to best channel that way of thinking into a rewarding career and life.

The brain is complex. It has an outer layer for rational thought and an inner layer for emotional processing. It has multiple cognitive drivers or so-called patterns. No two individuals think the same, not even twins. I was pursuant to knowing how I can align my work to the thinking tendencies that I have. Thought always precedes action. This is not challengeable. How you think will determine how you shall act.

Can I really know how I think? What is my 'brain design'? What is the type of work that best matches my cognitive abilities? Is behaviour predictable? Can we design a career path in high school that anticipates these functions well enough? Can we allow our thinking patterns to be developed and expanded?

The answer to all the questions above is *yes*, you definitely can. I did not leave a single psychometric tool unstudied in my research. I used about seventy-two tools on myself. I studied their basic methodology in detail. I have spoken to thousands of parents and teachers across the world, and have met a lot of career design enthusiasts.

I am a neuroscience fanatic. Well, for me, every day is like a date with the brain. I often exclaim in my seminars that it is my romance with the brain that keeps me going all day long.

INTRODUCTION

I was a victim of 'observer bias'. I observed my parents' careers (both in medicine) and jumped into this discipline without knowing the inner core of my brain's thinking type. I was a creator and innovator. I felt dry soon in my career, catering only to the patients. Each day was repetitive, dull, and boring. I felt accomplished, having been awarded thirteen gold medals and receiving a fat pay cheque, but never fulfilled.

I wanted to develop and work on a broad scale. Education and healthcare are the two pillars of humanity. The innovator/entrepreneur spirit was not allowing me to become complacent with my accomplishments. I will be frank and honest here. For the past eight years, there has not been a single weekend that I have had free to myself. The research for this book has been an eight-year-long journey. I am not tired but fuelled with a greater passion to now deliver this program to every single child on the planet. This desire aligns with my purpose-centric and innovative thinking brain type. This is the career synergy and success formula. You shall read about it more in the last bonus chapter.

I am a huge fan of whole-brain science proposed by Prof. Ned Herrmann and Prof. Dr. Kobus Neethling. This science has been instrumental in my life to help avoid the aftershocks that arise from not understanding people's behaviour, be it my boss, parents, friends, or colleagues. The science is so apt. The brain is divided into rational and limbic types. Rational is the thinking type and the limbic is the emotional seat. *Mybraindesign*® and the 'drivers of thinking' are re-worked versions of the whole-brain science but cater to career choices. The 'opportunity awareness quiz' and 'success signature experiments' are exclusively developed and dedicated to contributing cutting-edge information to the world beyond this known science.

Who is our main focus when we talk about a potential career choice? It is now Generation Alpha and whoever follows.

Generation Alpha (i.e., children born after 2010) are privileged and challenged at the same time. Over the course of my decade-long research, I have met thousands of parents. Most are worried about the future career choices of their children. They are struggling to catch up with the era. There are so many choices that even choosing the right option has become an analysis-paralysis affair for many.

Who should be picking up this book? If you are a parent, teacher, or adult struggling to identify the best-known career path for someone young, a post-college student struggling to fit or conform to your new degree, or a career counsellor helping others find their best career fit, this book is for you.

No science or scientific process is a fortune teller. Science is a dataset. A lot of reading between the lines is required. The logic can be the same but the interpretation of the logic can vary. We have hence built a pyramid (seven-level structure) to step out a successful career journey. Each level comes from years of dedicated research. I am grateful to my fellow researchers and colleagues for this book.

Neuroscience is both complex and easy at the same time. Complex until you do not get it right and simple once you get it right. I always exclaim that it is like mathematics. It seems puzzling when you do not get the right answer, though once solved, it is like a piece of cake.

If you are wondering whether this book offers yet another personality or aptitude assessment, let me clarify, it does not. Umpteen such tools are available on the internet, most for free, at least for the basic versions. There are commonly used tools in career choices such as the Holland Hexagon, MBTI®, Strong Interest Inventory®, and others. I have performed each of those and personally like them all. However, I am failing to understand the 'one-shot tells all' approach for the same persona. Yes, the basic tool provides an understanding of personality, behaviour, interests, and aptitude. But what next? How do we drive home an understanding of more than 800 careers (common ones as well) to children, and believe me, to parents and teachers too? This is the essence of the pyramid of career success. It begins with the self-discovery assessment with *Mybraindesign*® and self-development as a continuum.

Mybraindesign® is our proprietary tool. It comprises more than thirty-five questions and is delivered online. We have validated and aptly curated it to suit children and adults. It is the foundation and backbone of our process.

Opportunity awareness, which is the next stage in the pyramid, is presented as a supplementary brain career quest set quiz for the junior and senior levels, which is available online on various e-commerce stores (from Brainforia, our parent company). This opens the door of curiosity towards careers. Once you are subliminally or subconsciously exposed to the words, you start to engage with those in real life. Why do you think most kids who are questioned about their career choices end up answering only a few options – pilot, teacher, astronaut, or in today's era, a YouTuber? It is because their brains are in reality seeing these professions in their lessons, daily life, and around them. Why does no one talk about being a nanotechnologist? Because none of these lessons drive home the awareness for such careers. Children only reflect their immediate reality.

There are seventeen different types of thinking proposed in the book. These are metaphoric extensions of the modelled divisions of the brain. Each of us has a unique combination of thinking pattern. Well, is it that simple that each of us harbours just one of the seventeen types of thinking brain? The answer is very interesting and I would urge you to go through Chapters 6, 7, and 8 to understand this concept.

What Are the Remaining Chapters All About?

The first chapter is a showcase of my life, the real reason why I am writing this book. The second chapter gives a broad outline of the need for career discovery tools and the right age to undergo the same. Following this, Chapter 3 talks about the available career discovery tools.

A lot of interesting neuroscience facts are relayed in between so that one can take them from theoretical assumptions to practical applications. A lovely mascot, Sir Ebrall (derived from cerebral), will take us through this interesting relay of information.

While Chapters 3 and 4 are dedicated to understanding the brain type of the Generation Alpha and the world of work that exists in the 21st century. This is the era of the information superhighway, where there are more Wi-Fi spots than drinking water spots, and more screen time than green time. The Covid-19 pandemic has accelerated the technological transformation to the remotest parts of the world.

The forthcoming generation will have careers in emerging fields such as cyber security, cryptocurrency, digital business, data science, etc. They will be lifelong learners, holding multiple jobs across multiple careers. More than 50% of the jobs that exist today are predicted to be automated in the near future. Robots are no longer potential or feasible, they are already here.

We need to equip ourselves and up-level our game in understanding the relevant shifts and changing roles of the workplace so that we can become exposed to them at the right pace and make them slowly merge into the realities of the new digital world. We must be able to support them through the transition. Starting a dialogue about career choice early in high school is a *must*.

We need the schools to build an expanded curriculum showcasing the demands of tomorrow so that young brains are primed to anticipate even the unexpected. In doing this, parents have an even bigger role to play. Having the time to be involved in their children's decisions and discussions about the future is important.

The last three chapters (4, 5 and 6), focus on the concepts of extracurricular activity or hobby crafting for the kids. What kind of hobbies should be offered to high schoolers that can align with their career choices? What is the life-design blueprint for a final career choice?

Some of the successful people in various fields have had their brains mapped and the appendix provides a review of these brain profiles. We are chasing the ABC for career success — the anatomical, biological, and cognitive bases for career success. We are inviting the stalwarts in their career fields and mapping them for the *Mybraindesign*® and the actual thirty-two channel brain EEG. The experimentation to understand the default brain wiring using this sophisticated approach is ongoing and we will be happy to present some more of the data on our website on a continual basis.

We want more *Mybraindesign*® career enthusiasts. Join us in this journey together. We are glad to welcome you! Let the future be clear and bright not just for you and the young people under your care, but for the world at large. Clarity breeds confidence and confidence brings *success* — and this is what this book is all about.

1
Arranged-Cum-Love Career: What a Dilemma!

I love to offer the analogy of marriage when it comes to the dilemma of career choice. While arranged marriage in the western world may be unheard of, it remains a practice in many Asian countries. Arranged marriage is an institution where the boy and the girl do not opt to choose each other but their parents or siblings arrange the relationship. Career paths for children, when chosen years in advance by teachers, parents, peers, and sometimes grandparents, is an example of an arranged career. My career was chosen by my parents, both of whom were doctors. It's not that they were the dictators of my life, but because I had no clear picture of what I wanted to pursue even after finishing high school with fantastic marks, I entrusted the choice to them. Was this a wise move? Has everything in my life been great as a result of this choice?

We have two brains. One of them is a thinking rational brain while the other is a limbic or emotional brain. Simply put, one loves a fact as it is and the other loves the meaning of it. We are essentially a complex mixture of both in various proportions.

Let me introduce you to Sir Ebrall who shall guide us and teach us more about the fun facts of neuroscience. I bet you will love him.

Sir Ebrall

We have evolved from creepy-crawly creatures to anatomically modern humans with a ton of cerebral cortex or folds helping us make intelligent decisions. I am sure you shall be curious enough to find out more about it as you read through the book.

The 'Zero to Hero' Choice

I feel so naive thinking of the past now in that I had no clue of what my career could look like. The only thing that I had some hunch about was that I was a creator. I could build things. But building things leads to what careers? I had zero clue. I would go on any number of fieldtrips with my parents, be it to the airport, hotel, hospital, or thermal power station, and on return, I would recreate exactly the same scene. I would consider the minutest details. I would make use of all household items to make sure the place that I visited was recreated in my home in the exact way that I had seen it.

I had inbuilt leadership qualities that would allow me to gather a few children around my home and play some innovative and fun games. I was not afraid. I was always ready to experiment. I wanted to be a role model for other children. I was restless. I was quite intelligent and creative at the same time. I wanted to create something great, or rather anything great that could impact the lives of millions for good. This thought was constantly bothering me in my childhood. There was a feeling that my life was crafted to be a special purpose vehicle delivering something for the betterment and uplifting of people.

But I Had No Clue About My Career Choices or Life Choices

My parents were both in the medical field. I had fantastic marks in science at high school. My mother and I went to every person who could guide us in selecting the right career path. There were no career counsellors about twenty-six years back. There was no concept of a personality test. I had opted for the one and only aptitude assessment in Mumbai, India, about sixteen hours from my hometown. I was no Generation Alpha (i.e., born between the early 2010s and early 2020s) with access to the online information superhighway. I grew up without a mobile phone, laptop, television, or any form of advanced scientific assessment at my high school. The common dictum was if you score good marks you take up science and if not you opt for commerce.

There was a choice of pursuing a career in medicine or civil engineering. I was one of the top scholars in the state and was offered a scholarship to study in Singapore. Luckily, I had visited Singapore in my early teens and I could imagine what my life could be like in that country. The dilemma of choosing which career to follow was profound. Practising medicine could be done across the street in my hometown, while pursuing engineering would mean travelling to another state or country.

Medicine was offered free of cost to girls in my state. I didn't have to pay a dime to become a doctor. Economically, however, both the options matched. To choose between engineering and medicine was like picking an orange or apple just by the mere look of it. I had no clue about engineering although I had seen my distant uncle working as a civil engineer. The field of medicine was closely observed due to my parents' inclination and engagement in that field.

The Title Fight: Dr. or Er?

What did I finally end up choosing? You must be wondering. The dilemma was quite disturbing. On the one hand, there was engineering and on the other end medicine. I can still remember the time of day when right at the last hour the bell rang and I was called for my final choice. The stress of that final hour was so immense that it formed a rock-solid memory in my brain. Life seemed so fragile for a moment, frenzied with fear of making the wrong choice. All the 'what if' questions were popping like lilies in the brain.

My whole family went into a unique intellectual drama followed by the trauma of the choice. I ended up doing medicine. You could say the choice went well. I was the most comfortable student in medicine. I used to be the hero of the class. I could memorise anatomy and physiology so well that professors used to talk about setting a unique paper challenging my understanding. I was like a fish in water. I was at the top of my graduation class and had the luxury to choose my postgraduate path.

Because I had no fine motor skills and it was clear that I could not be a surgeon. Internal or general medicine was my only love and finishing it was a piece of cake . I was a topper all throughout my career in medicine with over thirteen gold medals/prizes. I was very hardworking and diligent in my endeavours to learn medicine. I pursued five years of a Bachelor of Medicine, Bachelor of Surgery (MBBS), which is a basic medical degree followed by a three-year postgraduate degree in medicine (MD).

There is Always More to Medicine

The real-life post-MD medicine started and I found myself again questioning the future. Having an MD was not enough for me. I wanted to challenge myself to the best available course in medicine. My intelligence wanted to play with fire. Neurology was considered to be the most difficult subject for most students. Even good students dreaded neurology cases. But I like to take challenges head-on. The funniest part of my career journey is that the choice of neurology was a mere accident. My roommate was so passionate about neurology that she used to bombard me with questions on neurology pretty much each day and night. I had no choice but to listen to her forced teachings. Destiny played hard. She could not opt for the seat due to family issues while I was able to join the super-specialty program almost immediately. I still remember her vivid expression of congratulating me to live her dream. I was so taken aback at the news of her not being able to pursue neurology. Again, man proposes but God can dispose of it. This makes you wonder and delve into many other philosophical questions.

My journey in neurology for about four years was unique and exciting. I met some fantastic people as teachers and friends. I was able to understand that the brain is my first love. I was awe-struck by the sheer power of the brain. I was more inclined to know the physiology of the brain's functions than to limit myself to fixing broken brains. I really want to kindle the normal lives to lead a path of glory and success.

Neuroscience has hidden gems. Knowing how your brain works can make you tap its maximum potential powers. The mascot Sir Ebrall shall be giving us a lot of tips throughout the book and will teach us more about the brain.

My Life in a Nutshell

Somebody has rightly said 'Life is all about choices we make'. The decisions we take every single day, big or small, impact our lives in one way or another and determine how our coming years shall unfold. To summarise my journey across the five continents today sounds so easy. I completed my master's degree in medicine and neurology in Mumbai, India. I further completed my stroke fellowship in Calgary, Canada. I worked in central Africa for a few years. I pursued a Master of Business Administration (MBA) at Cambridge, UK. I had a summer stint with the United Nations Non-Communicable Disease (UNNCD) program in Geneva. For the last several years I have been based in Dubai, United Arab Emirates (UAE), working as a medical director and a specialist neurologist for RAK Hospital.

Now you may be wondering how a degree in business (MBA) came up in the career of a neurologist and specialist in paralytic stroke medicine. You asked the right question. I was accomplished but not content. After finishing all these studies, I still had questions lingering in my mind. Am I going to deliver to the world my passion? Am I steering my career path to the best of my abilities? Will I be working on a larger scale?

Life is all about purpose and meaning. Within me was a burning passion to work on a broad scale. An impact so big that many lives had to be touched by my work. The options in front of me were clear – research, working as an entrepreneur, author/teacher, and working for a small organisation creating a big impact. Later you will realise these options exactly match the four sides of the brain's process drivers.

I never wanted a typical nine-to-five job. I wanted excitement, to travel and meet new people, to create new programs that could impact people at large. I quickly understood being a neurologist was not going to give me any of the above. The path to experimentation was unclear. Pursuing a very traditional neurology career and trying now to work on a much broader scale? This plan itself sounded like a pun. I was sure I wanted to do the extraordinary out of the neurology career. **I knew the *why*, but I did not know the *how*.**

Do you Follow Destiny or Does it Follow You?

I always wondered who follows – do you follow destiny or does destiny follow you? This is a deep philosophical question. This book, however, is not about this question. This book is a testimony to the navigation across the choices in one's career path. The crossroads in my own career and the experiment of navigating a path from medicine to neurology to stroke medicine to an MBA testify to this effort.

I was a hard worker all throughout my career. After becoming an accomplished neurologist I realised there was something missing in my life. Yes, I was earning very well. I could get jobs across the globe. I had the flexibility of choices. There were only about 5,000 stroke specialists around the world when I graduated. The demand-supply ratio was highly skewed. I could go back to India and pursue a private career establishing my own centre. Or, I could easily stay in Canada and pursue a research path.

Money is Not Everything in Life

The luxury of the choices was immense. How many of you reading the book feel accomplished with great pay cheques but feel empty within? You feel that you are meant to do something completely different and derive your joy from something that is far removed from your current job role.

Upon deep reflection over the course of six months and taking up about seventy-two psychometric tests through hundreds of Google sites, some free but mostly paid for, I understood that I am indeed a creator. I am a rebel. I love to invent. I love to build and develop. I like to experiment. I blew thousands of dollars meeting hundreds of career coaches and doing multiple analyses and tests in the pursuit of finding my true purpose. I have loads of test results in my house. This was the time immediately following my fellowship for stroke neurology. I took a complete six-month break. *I wanted to be sure of my next go-to path.*

The analysis of self-discovery was profound. It clearly set the path of my life. For once, I was convinced that the childhood hunch was indeed true. I am meant to create a mission-driven business that can upscale to reach thousands of people.

Working on my self-discovery led me to an idea about reshaping and developing the tools and/or processes that would enable me to help many students and people stuck in their careers. Science helped me de-clutter my own career path. I was convinced that the formula could help so many others stuck in their own career paths. I started to experiment with one of the tools of whole-brain science helping me to derive cognitive preferences. I started to work on something that I had no idea would take a mammoth shape. I had to work on a huge sample size. I needed to validate the tool statistically. I was very fortunate to have some great mentors in the process.

Having a Purpose in Life is Magical

My purpose was sealed. It was clear that I would be working to help the young school-goers find their best path forward. New energy pulsed down my spine to wake me every single day towards this goal. While I carried on with my research about the science of career choices, I had some social pressures. My mother went through post-operative depression which took a toll on my family. I was the sole breadwinner at that point in time when my father had to leave his work to support my mother. We experienced quite difficult years then. I had no option but to join a traditional nine-to-five job again in Mumbai. But believe me, I was terrified of working in a traditional setting. There was no excitement. I felt stifled despite being paid well. The urge to not sit in one place without experimentation was becoming more intense day after day. I was struggling to keep my feelings at bay. However, I was pulling each day praying I could be back to experimentation and do something completely out of the ordinary. Once my family problems began to settle after a year, I decided to put my CV on LinkedIn, which was quite a new baby on board in India. I asked to join any country that could give me a challenging non-traditional job role in neurology or stroke medicine.

I received a call from a man within two days of posting my CV. He invited me for an interview without disclosing where the job would be located. He was a stunning man, clad in a black suit and tie. He was well-spoken and asked me for a compensation plan. I was so fed up with India that I threw a number twenty times my salary at the time. My friend who had accompanied me looked at my face in awe. She must have been wondering whether I had lost my marbles or if I was trying to pitch the ball out of the court.

To our utter surprise, the man agreed to that price. Until about an hour into the interview, there was no clue where the job was and what kind of job it was. Of course, it was related to neurology, but in what capacity, and where?

He finally declared that his hospital was in Kinshasa, Democratic Republic of Congo, Africa. I immediately looked at my friend and asked have you heard the name of the country? She silently whispered, no. While the discussion was now all about the ease and facility which would be provided in Congo, I was in two minds. I asked for some time to conduct my due diligence. The first response from anyone who heard my story exclaimed I was crazy. They said that enough jobs existed in India and why would I leave my family and go all the way to central Africa? They were fearful of wars, malaria, and other communicable diseases.

I started to research more about the central African region. I was excited to go to a new place and meet new people. I soon learned that French was compulsory to be able to join the job. I had no knowledge of French and the only way to learn the language was to start watching French movies. I started to do that silently without telling my family. My friends were not a party to my plan either. Obviously, who would agree a few years back to pack bags for a country that was war-stricken?

The Silent Gene Speaks Up One Day

I was very happy in my new role in Africa. I met some of the most inspiring people in my life. I was so very welcomed to the country. I fell in love with the natural resources that the country offered. I could see hundreds of patients a day, travel to far and deep places, and eat some exotic foods. I never once felt out of place. While I was enjoying the work, I still was brewing the hunger for taking my research to the next level. The deep urge to bring out my career science choice research to the world in the form of a scalable and social business started to haunt me. I constantly worked on the weekends towards that goal. I never took a weekend off, yet never felt drained as the research gave me enough fire to run for the next week. I started to do pop-ups (unlike start-ups) – small entrepreneurial stints to support the idea. I opened a company and was joined by my then friend-cum-teacher. The experiments led me to gain exposure to the entrepreneurial demands and nuances.

The Human Brain is New Each Day

I have always believed that pushing new boundaries is the driving purpose of the human brain. We have not stopped creating since the beginning of evolution. Our brains have constantly been hunting new pastures. How could I be complacent sitting all day and doing a nine-to-five job? My brain was not at ease accepting this daily plan. I had no fortune or other skills to make a venture in India successful. The side hustle taught me that my skills were far short of my dreams.

One Message Was Very Loud and Clear. I Had to Upskill. I Needed to Learn Management Skills. I Had to Do an MBA.

I started researching the business schools and it was very clear that I should pursue an MBA from a top college in the world. I was dissuaded by my colleagues that I was too old for business school. Yes, medical science involves many years of study. Why would a school reject me merely for my age? I was committed to learning management skills so that I could create a revolution in the science of self-discovery. I applied to the Massachusetts Institute of Technology (MIT), Oxford, Stanford, Cambridge, IE Business School, and Institut Européen d'Administration des Affaires (INSEAD). I had to redo the Graduate Management Admission Test (GMAT) exam after many years of being out of touch with mathematics and English. I had to learn from scratch how to present my dreams in essay form so that I could kickstart my journey into one of the top MBA schools. I was accepted at IE, Cambridge, and HEC Paris and waitlisted at MIT. My dream was coming true, slowly but surely.

My Dream Comes True

Receiving a letter of acceptance from Cambridge with scholarship was the best thing in my life. The ambition of doing an MBA after a very long medicine career was indeed not an easy one. I was about to take up something where I may not be successful. I was about to challenge many people's advice that it was foolish to invest money and a year of my life in studying a new discipline after all my years at the grindstone in medicine. It is easy to live other people's dreams but to live one's own dream takes courage and grit. People may want something out of you but what you wish for and want is the crucial thing in life.

I Was Finally Not Just a Brain Plumber

I thoroughly enjoyed the MBA program. I was able to navigate my way through corporate finance with ease alongside most other subjects I had never before studied. It was a true calling. I could immediately draw my own plan that in the medium-term I would lead an organisation and in the long-term work on my research to impact millions globally. I kept my entrepreneurial spirit alive throughout the course and in the process learned a lot. I was able to meet so many inspiring people in life. Although the Covid-19 pandemic hit during the last term making contact learning impossible, Zoom allowed it all to happen virtually.

Cambridge is Magical

Cambridge is a beautiful city and the Judge Business School is one of its most magical places. I always say magical places bring magic to your life. Cambridge is one such place. The one year at Cambridge opened the pathway for management and executive leadership in the UAE and gave me all the right skills to pursue my dream of impacting lives on a broad scale.

All's Well That Ends Well

My real calling is to help children who are confused about their career prospects. I was able to translate all my research into a program called *Mybraindesign*®. My real-life career insights led me to develop the seven levels of success for a career choice. I finally embarked on the journey that I feel I am meant to deliver in this lifetime. I want to be the torchbearer of a revolution in finding the purpose for young teenagers or high school students.

Legacy for Life in Career Choice Science

This book is the product of my constant search for finding the right career path through self-discovery. I have been working relentlessly for over eight years to develop the formula, since the time of realising my career discontentment. I have interviewed thousands of parents and students in the process of my self-discovery. I was part of all the career forums in the world. I studied every single test with the finest of details. I took interviews with successful people in various fields and mapped their brain preferences. *Mybraindesign*® was a research effort that lasted eight long years. It was refined time and again. It was perfected with effort.

Ikigai: Mine to Yours – the Final Summary

This book and the accompanying program are a testimony to the work of a desperate entrepreneur who was searching for her own *Ikigai*-purpose in life. *Ikigai* is a Japanese word. It essentially refers to something that gives a person a sense of person, a reason for living. I had no idea that doing the research for my own career would lead me to design a program for high school and college graduates worldwide. My enthusiasm knew no bounds when a lot of schools and other career counselling centres started to value my work. They opted to commission me and the team for career coaching worldwide. My vision solidified and I would become a pioneer in building a school for future readiness.

Success and Contentment May Not Go Hand in Hand

While being content is to definitely be successful, being successful may not require one to be content. This was a strong message for my own life. I always felt that the science of self-discovery could help anyone who wished to create magic in their life. The *Mybraindesign*® program and the career science methodology can impact the lives of millions of children. Understanding the cognitive preferences and navigating life through conscious decisions is key.

Learning the fundamentals of neuroscience has been a key pillar of my success. I always exclaim, *it is my romance with the brain.* Neuroscience has a lot that remains unexplored, and while much has already been discovered, this is not delivered to the world in simple formula sets. This book allows me to present the neuroscience-based processes for helping the Generation Alphas choose a career fit for their brain preferences.

The World Needs Magical Bagpipers to Lead as We Move Through the 21st Century.

My idea is plain and simple. When you work in a profession or towards a purpose that fits your brain preferences, you will create magic. I worked on my best brain preferences and finally chose a purpose-driven mission in life. I had to navigate through rough waters. I want to make those waters calm and smooth for you. Let us start the journey together. I am excited and I hope you are too!

Walk the Talk

1. **Visioneering.** Sit comfortably. Close your eyes and picture yourself on a forward time scale. Where do you see yourself in five years, ten years, and fifteen years? What are you doing? Who is around you? What have you created? Who is celebrating your existence? What is the world's reaction? How are you feeling?

   Sir Ebrall's tip: The brain cannot differentiate between a real and visualised event. Repeatedly doing this exercise will, therefore, make the brain believe the truth and indeed you can be that. This is the power of *visioneering* – nothing but the secret behind Rhonda Byrnes' *Secret*.

   If you are a parent, do the same exercise for your children. Think of where you see them in five years, ten years, and

fifteen years. Make them do the same exercise. Of course, they may think anything radical which is completely fine.
2. **What is your personal SWOT?** Describe your strengths, weaknesses, opportunities, and threats, that impact your career. Punch at least 5 points in each section.

Storyselling. Storytelling is very powerful. In fact, storytelling is also story*selling*. We are all salespeople. Daniel Pink reinforces the same idea in his book *'To Sell is Human'*. I am selling healthy eating and exercise every single day to my patients. What are you selling? You can share with us your career victory story at www.mybraindesign.org

2

What's all the Fuss About Career Discovery?

Elaborate Life-Role Counselling Will Supersede Limited Career Counselling for the Forthcoming Generation

> 'The world of work is not a straightforward career ladder as it was years ago. It is more like a jungle gym.'
>
> — ROBERT SHEA

The world is undergoing dynamic and rapid change. The technological leaps we are witnessing are uncanny. The industrial 4.0 revolution, i.e., the era that will be led by digital technologies, is sweeping the world. This revolution represents a fundamental change in the way we live, work and relate to each other.

The era is merging the physical, digital, and biological worlds in ways that will create huge opportunities and some dangers.

When we look at the world of work, and the way young people will soon experience it, this becomes obvious. Process-mediated jobs are already being lost to new-age robots. Previously unheard jobs such as drone operators, big data detectives, personal data brokers, genetic diversity officers, digital tailors, personal memory curators, virtual store Sherpas, chief trust officers, and ethical sourcing officers are all around the corner. Some traditional career types are going to slowly become redundant. Understanding these rapid shifts and further embracing the careers that are driven by an inclusive human-centred future is the need of the hour.

Members of Generation Alpha (and the late Generation Z, born between 1997 and 2012), are going to face a major trend shift. In particular, there will be a shortening of the lifecycle of organisations and businesses. Full-time employment will slowly transition into short-term contractual and project-based engagements. There will be a rise in the so-called hybrid workforce and gig economy. Knowledge-based jobs will be overtaken by innovative jobs. Helping to prepare today's youth to understand these changes and align their skills correctly during high school is essential.

The pyramid of career design encompassing *Mybraindesign®* and *lifedesign blueprint®* is constructed to help children understand the coming change of pace during their high school years. My passion for self-discovery led me to pivot to the best career of my life. The neuroscience-based process allows a deep-dive inquiry into the brain's powers so that adequate upskilling is planned by the stakeholders towards the best career choices well in advance. While the stakeholders can be parents or teachers, they can also be other role models in the child's life. For me, my spiritual teacher was a role model and guide.

I believe that so-called career counselling will be superseded by life counselling, which is not provided as a one-off test but as a dedicated curriculum in the high school system across the globe. This book is our small effort towards implementing this mammoth change.

By the end of this book, you will understand why we aim to urge the parents and teachers to start the process of life counselling early in high school. Tapping the potential of the brains of the generation by making them aware of the immense power which lies inside them is necessary. As the stakeholders – parents, teachers, and career counsellors – we are the torchbearers for this shift.

By providing a scientific overview of the career choice discovery process that we follow, we are paving the way for a smooth and seamless integration for Generation Alpha into the new world of work.

But before moving on, I am sure you may be reading and wondering, is career choice a real problem? Why do we need to be so fixated on finding the right career choice? There are tons of career counsellors and methods available, some are free on the internet, why go through one more career discovery method? Let me help you navigate these aptly raised questions throughout the chapter.

What is the Real Problem?

Globally, the majority of high schoolers and the minority of university students are confused about their career paths. Often, they seek help from tools to guide them in the best career choice either online or through their school or university career guidance. In doing this, they use the help of personality, aptitude, interests, and psychometric tests. The 21st century is dynamic and choices are changing each single day. Allowing only the age-old assessment tools such as aptitude and personality into a new environment does not fit well.

While these tools have their own merits and demerits, the fundamental science behind them is often not translated into daily practice. I have also seen multiple tools being used for career advice while they are not meant for this purpose.

I have seen a lot of students starting this inquiry late in their high school years. There is also inertia in this regard from the parents, while they wait for the 'right time' to fix the dilemma.

In My Opinion, the Right Time Was Yesterday and Not Today for Exploring the Career Choices

A lot of teachers and parents leave the career decisions to the discriminatory choices of the children. This is completely non-scientific and impractical from a neurodevelopmental standpoint. It is like leaving them to choose the medicines that they fathom to be right for a physical illness. We all take time to find our feet. It is a fine balance between suggesting and aiding the child to choose a career versus dictating the choices. Rather than leaving the decision or dictating it, the best way is to instil a mature and sensible mindset with complete self-discovery assistance so that appropriately informed decisions can be made.

 **Sir Ebrall's tip:** The frontal lobes are not myelinated until adolescence. The myelin sheath is a cover around the brain nerve cells. Myelination is important for cognitive development. The executive skill development,

planning, reasoning, and decision-making are all due to the well-myelinated frontal portions of the brain. Remember it is not myelinated until about twenty-five years of age. If your teenage child is throwing a temper tantrum and has impulse control issues, do not worry. The process is not complete until about twenty-five years.

Is Career Choice This Complex?

Well, you may be wondering about this question. Why not just base the decision on their main interests? Why do we need to think so much about our career choices? Finally, as the child discovers their interests over time, the career choice or selection will eventually fall into place.

While it is not as simple as it sounds, the answer to the section question lies in the vast and practical neuroscience literature. A meta-analysis study suggests that vocational interests showed substantial continuity over time from early adolescence to middle adulthood. Interest stability remained unchanged during much of adolescence and increased dramatically during the college years (eighteen to twenty-one) where it then remained for two decades. (1) Hence, early life interests are quite variable. I am sure most of you would have heard children talking about becoming pilots, astronauts, YouTubers(the new age), chefs, etc. Every week they have something new to talk about. This is very natural.

My work suggests that we have to reverse engineer the process and keep the interests for the last stage before we seal the deal. If we start with interests, we will lose the opportunity to explore the various potential career capabilities revealed by the brain's inherent cognitive processes or strengths. We also lose the opportunity for self-discovery in the process.

Interests Are Important and Cannot Be Ignored

Interest definitely prompts learning. It takes a hell of an effort to do something that one is not interested in compared to what they find interesting. Give me a book to read and I am happy as hell. Give me something to cook, and I will run to the farthest corner of my house. The main function of interest is to promote curiosity and keep motivation. Interest is central to intrinsic motivation. The brain feels dull and heavy when bored or frustrated. These negative feelings get in the way of job satisfaction. They are also avoidance states that keep the person away from his or her goal.

Sir Ebrall's tip: When you are struggling in a state of boredom, just play the *interest* magic game. Give five minutes to any task your brain enjoys and believe me, it will be reset. This exercise will kickstart enough chemicals to keep you going. If you are in this state right now, go do something interesting for five minutes and come back. You will know for sure what I am talking about. Neuroscience suggests that interest is self-replenishing. In other words, being interested in something not only uses up the precious cognitive reserves but also promotes the restoration of these resources. Positive feelings and loads of happy chemicals get boosted when one does something interesting.

Interest is a coping resource in the brain-power toolkit that you can call on when needed.

Start Early, Start Right!

Fundamentally, the brain can be stretched to work the way you train it. If self-discovery is performed at an early and appropriate age, transitioning to the world of work can be seamless. The majority of students start the exercise of self- and career discovery at the far end of their high school education, by which time there is very little space left to hone the extra skills necessary to adopt a certain career path. Our clear and loud message to the world through this work is that **we need to start early and start right!**

Clarity From the Start is a Must

The only way to overcome the shortcomings of the career discovery path so that a new generation is capable of adapting to the new world of work is to start early providing them with the framework of various careers in a simple and easy method during their early high school years. My team has worked hard to shape the pyramid for career success for high schoolers.

One has to provide subconscious information multiple times to relay it properly to the conscious brain. Making students aware of the various careers can be achieved in a fun and interactive way so that they can start noticing the subtle world of work around them.

I have met so many students when conducting my research who have barely been able to list seven to ten career choices in their career vocabulary. There are more than 800 major career paths and children are barely aware of a handful. It was surprising to discover this. Despite the availability of YouTube and the Google search engine, this was the state of their awareness. I often wonder what if I had been exposed to the choices beyond medicine and engineering, would I have opted for something else. **Ask this question for yourself and try to discover your core calling.**

The Pace in the Chase is a Must

The pace of change is unbelievable. Catching up to this pace by Generation Alpha children will need a dedicated approach to self-discovery and self-analysis early on, so that they can also understand their personal behaviours and those of the changing world and its demands. The idea of the career design process is fundamental to accelerating this pace into this chase.

Knowing How to Think is More Important Than What to Think

Knowing how we think is more important than what we think. Teaching children to understand how they think and how others think is required. While our system is backed by the fundamentals of neuroscience and whole-brain science, a lot of it is experiential having evolved over the years. Our elaborate interviews with parents, teachers, and the students led us to understand the real gap. Knowing about one's personal strengths is necessary. It is also important to learn the techniques to overcome any resistance or rigidity in one's thinking.

The personal SWOT (strengths, weaknesses, opportunities, and threats) is a popular though outdated tool in applying to the self because one must convert every threat to an opportunity with a heroic mindset due to the demands of the 21st century.

With the demands of the jobs of tomorrow, one will need to tap into all the available powers of the self. The competition for jobs is going to be fierce.

A survey by Pearson found that seven in ten workers are in jobs where there is greater uncertainty about the future. Their findings also confirm the importance of higher-order cognitive skills such as complex problem-solving, originality, fluency of ideas, and active learning. These will be the most in-demand skills for the future. (2)

We have developed a new tool focusing on the demands of tomorrow that we call SORT. The tool showcases strengths, opportunities, resistance to growth, and the techniques to overcome this resistance right from high school. Let us draw a career SORT chart (Figure 1).

Strengths	Opportunities
Narrate all your career strengths. E.g., you could be good at analysis, process understanding, designing, selling, manufacturing, leadership, etc.	Identify career advancement opportunities due to your strengths. You might be promoted as a manager, for example, because of your exceptional quality of leadership.
Resistance (to growth)	Techniques (to overcome resistance)
Identify the weaknesses in your career. e.g., you might not be a good speaker, are introverted, don't like taking risks, don't like to analyse, etc.	List the techniques and extracurricular skills to overcome the resistance. Let's say you join a speaking club and improve your confidence.

FIGURE 1. QUADRANT DIAGRAM OF THE FOUR SORT FIELDS.

Let me give an example of my SORT map to drive home the point. I love neuroscience. I love fixing the brain. My cognitive-thinking style presents a strength in creativity and process-driven work. But I detest talking to people, which is my biggest resistance. I am essentially an introvert but my job demands developing a trustworthy relationship with my patients. I understand my resistance and have taken all the steps needed to overcome it. I joined a speaker's club, learned to talk in public, and took lessons to improve my presentation style. The book is also a testimonial to overcoming the resistance I had by talking to people. I decided to not just sit behind the closed doors assessing the data being a neuroscientist but to outgrow my former self and embrace the world to take the message of self-discovery far and wide.

The Pyramid of Career Choice Success – Career Success Blueprint

The brain is essentially complex and no amount of simplification can justify the workings of this organ. I wanted to really craft a simple approach to defining the process of achieving career choice success. This system does not claim to be comprehensive and ultra-specific in finding the right career direction through neuroscience concepts. It is a sincere attempt to simplify and explore the concept of career choices and provide rational steps towards the choice. No system is perfect. No psychometric tool (showcasing the personality or behaviour through a self-inquiry questionnaire) is completely accurate. Yet, building a system that is near perfect, or at least one that covers the major areas of focus, is what we have strived for.

The development of a pyramid system of career discovery with seven fundamental levels, which is simple and futuristic, is the output of years of research and hands-on tests involving thousands of students worldwide.

The Pyramid of Career Choice Success Stretches Beyond High School to College Students and Adults

Our methodology revolves around the simple fundamentals of the working brain. The brain's operating system is simple and complex at the same time. We want to fundamentally draw out the cognitive preferences and layout the choices mapped to the career clusters. Each section of the pyramid entails an evaluation and further discovery plan (see Figure 2). The whole process can be started from Grade 7 of high school, irrespective of the study curriculum. The process has no limitation in terms of the subjects or academics. This is a fundamental skeletal process for any child.

FIGURE 2. THE PYRAMID OF CAREER CHOICE (DIAGRAM BY THE AUTHOR).

Sneak Peek into *Mybraindesign*®

The brain has evolved from its primitive to rational or neocortex state over the years. The rational brain is all about the outer cortex where there is logic, understanding, and capability to perform complex cognitive tasks. While the limbic brain is all about emotions and processing of people and situations.

The *Mybraindesign*® provides a preferential map of the thinking abilities of the individual. It performs a descriptive, nonjudgmental analysis with no output or preferences being better or worse. There is no ranking or superior/inferior potential. The values or beliefs, attitudes, actions, interests, behaviour, and personality can all be efficiently derived from the brain design pattern.

The Thinking Flow Systems: From *What* to *Why* to *How*

It is not just important to understand the cognitive styles but also the flow of thinking patterns in the brain. We have designed each of the **flow maps** in response to this need. The seventeen different brain design flow maps can be assigned to each individual. Further archetypes/drivers of thinking can be integrated into the cognitive flow maps.

We have spent years formulating the career clusters. There are major and minor clusters. Major clusters are related to each of the seventeen brain designs while the minor clusters are related to the archetypes/drivers of thinking. The chapters on each of the sections shall clarify the concepts.

The 'Big Four'

While there are thousands of careers, it is very interesting that there are only four fundamental life paths that a person embraces. We have categorised all the careers under these four paths, which we call the 'big four'.

The big four career types are:
1. Data-centric – data scientist, data analyst, data consultant
2. Innovation-centric – entrepreneur, artist, creative designers

3. People-centric – medicine, nursing, marketing, public relations, social work
4. Process-centric – teaching, training, operations, event management

The jobs are divided into:
1. Research and discovery
2. Teaching/training and coaching
3. Management and organisation (middle to senior)
4. Enterprise or entrepreneurial-related activities

The Basic Science Behind the *Lifedesign Blueprint*®

The Kurt Lewin model of behaviour function is popular. Our fundamentals are based on his simple equation 'B = f(P, E)'. This states that an individual's behaviour (B) is a function (f) of the person (P), including their personality and motivation, and their environment (E), which includes both their physical and social surroundings.

The child growing up in Africa, having limited access to career choices, is different from the one growing up in America with easy to acquire and elaborate options. Hence considering the family values, background, financial position, and availability of resources is necessary for the career evaluation. The academic potential of the child or individual, the accessible skills, and the extracurricular support provided in the school are necessary to prescribe the right path forward. This is what our *lifedesign blueprint*® summarises for the child.

Our process starts with *Mybraindesign*®, a self-discovery assessment, and ends with a *lifedesign blueprint*® that completely navigates through all the factors influencing the career choices. Finally, it also allows adopting a plan for developing extracurricular skills on an ongoing basis.

Carol Dweck has studied the mindset types in great detail. (3) There are two main mindsets with which we can navigate life: 'growth' and 'fixed' mindsets. Having a growth mindset is essential for success. There is no doubt that Generation Alpha is not anticipated to harbour a fixed mindset. They shall be driven by authentic purpose-driven work and they are going to live even longer than the previous generation indicating the need for identifying their alignment to the world of work. But it is our duty to see that we are appropriately helping them to navigate through the rough seas of change. The stakeholders might also have to adopt a growth mindset in the process.

Without knowing how they think will not allow us to intervene in the way they can think better. It is important that we understand the way their brains are wired. A simple understanding will go a long way in taking the right steps in their career journeys. By the way, my most wonderful moments are when I am talking to the Generation Alphas. They are so full of life and enthusiasm. Adulthood is merely a step-by-step destruction of the ingenious creativity of the brains of children. I enjoy being in their company. Teaching them is like learning too. I am sure you can relate to what I am talking about.

Into the Shoes of Generation Alpha

Having grown up with the technological know-how, having lived a comfortable life (reared by relatively wealthy Millennials), having the world as a global village, and having the accessibility of data and information in microseconds is both a boon and a curse at the same time. Understanding the workings of the Generation Alpha brain is not an easy task. The stakeholders have to be super agile and cautious of the pace. Having a basic understanding of their brain wiring can go a long way in handling their behaviours.

The next chapter focuses on dissecting the brain behaviours of Generation Alpha. It is important for us to first dive into their premature or growing brains before we can talk about the pyramid of career choice and success discovery. Let us do that together. I bet it will be fun. But before that, you can also do some practical reflections.

Walk the Talk

1. Draw your career SORT chart. What are your strengths in your career and opportunities for success in the same? Kindly mention the resistance that you have faced and the ways in which you think you can overcome it (mention some extracurricular activities that can help you overcome the resistance).
2. Big four careers expansion – we have provided some examples in the chapter. A good resource to learn about the various career paths is www.bachelorsportal.com, where you can draw out more courses related to each of the big four career options. You can also browse our *careerpik* library on the website at www.mybraindesign.org
3. Is managing teenagers a real problem? How many of you have undergone this so-called 'teenache' (a headache dealing with teenagers)?

References

1. Hoff, K. A., Chu, C., Einarsdóttir, S., Briley, D. A., Hanna, A., & Rounds, J. (2022). Adolescent vocational interests predict early career success: Two 12-year longitudinal studies. *Applied Psychology, 71*, 49–75. doi:10.1111/apps.12311.
2. Pearson's research into the potential trends of a future work/employment environment can be found at https://www.simplilearn.com/future-of-work-article.
3. More than thirty years ago, Carol Dweck and her colleagues became interested in student attitudes about failure. That is how the terms 'fixed' and 'growth' mindsets were born. See the video by Carol Dweck at www.mindsetworks.com.

3
The Who, What, When, Where and How of Generation Alpha

Generation Alpha is a Generation That is Both Privileged and Challenged at the Same Time

> 'Never help a child with a task at
> which he feels he can succeed.'
>
> — MARIA MONTESSORI

Stephen Covey, author of the acclaimed *The 7 Habits of Highly Effective People*, offers the following quote: 'Seek first to understand than to be understood'. We are undergoing a massive generational transition. The generational shift from the silent generation (born before 1945) to Generation Alpha is quite vivid. Understanding the behaviours, attitudes, and workings of Generation Alphas is a herculean task. The current median age of the global population is merely thirty years. By December 2024, two billion people on the planted will have been born after 2010 to form Generation Alpha.

I presume that most of us reading this book would either be Generation Y (1977–1995) or Generation Z (born after 1996). Let me put forth some fun imagination exercises for you. What picture are you drawing about attitudes towards work and life for the incubating Generation Alpha? What manners and ways pop out in front of your eyes as you stretch your imagination further? Currently, children between the ages of eight and twelve are labelled tweens, and are a mixture of Generation Z and Generation Alpha. Social media is an integral part of the tween identity.

I am sure you will conjure images of children being glued to their devices, impatient, headstrong, and somewhat entitled. You pictured them quite well. App-based play, increased screen time, shorter attention spans and advanced digital literacy classifies them.

Categorically, what picture is being drawn for their world of work? Can you think about what kinds of jobs they would be aspiring to do? What kinds of jobs will exist in 2040? The World Economic Forum (WEF) states that 65% of jobs in the future will be ones that we have never heard of yet. (1)

New Era, New Ways of Defining Career Choices

They will have careers in emerging fields such as cybersecurity, cryptocurrency, digital business, etc. They will be lifelong learners, holding multiple jobs across multiple careers. Will the existing career tools allow them to understand these nuances? Our research suggests mere personality, aptitude, and interest inventories (commonly performed evaluations) are not going to help advance the children's understanding of their future careers.

Let us think a little deeper. Is the change new or unique to this era? The answer is very clear and apt. No, the change is not new. The only difference is that the speed and scope of the change are quite radical. We, the stakeholders of their future, will have to prepare Generation Alpha to adapt and thrive. Having more robots than humans in the workplace, exchanging crypto salaries, and enjoying business meetings in the hyperloop (travelling at the speed of 550 miles per hour) is no longer far from reality.

This is the era of the information superhighway. There are more Wi-Fi spots than drinking water spots; there is more screen time than green time. The pandemic has accelerated the technological transformation to the remotest places in the world. Babies born during the pandemic have been labelled as 'coronials'. The questions raised around the coronials' mental stability and the memories of the lockdowns are genuine. Will there be some deep psychosocial impact lingering over the years as they outgrow the pandemic? Only time shall tell with some of these questions.

**Time to ponder:** Will the temporal or so-called memory lobes be redundant as Google takes over? Will there be neural pathways that stretch to compete with humanised robots? Will there be thinking patterns that may be newly wired to adapt to the constant upgrades in technology? Will there be rapid evolutionary changes in brain circuitry where more of the soft skills or empathy will be harnessed?

No Doubt They Are Privileged

Generation Alphas are definitely privileged. They are starting their hierarchical needs as defined by the famous Maslow's pyramid much above the base of the pyramid. We can safely presume that they are starting two levels above the base. Figure 3 demonstrates Maslow's pyramid. They are going to be smarter than their counterparts. Already, studies have highlighted that the technological knowledge of an eight-year-old far surpasses the technological knowledge of his or her parents.

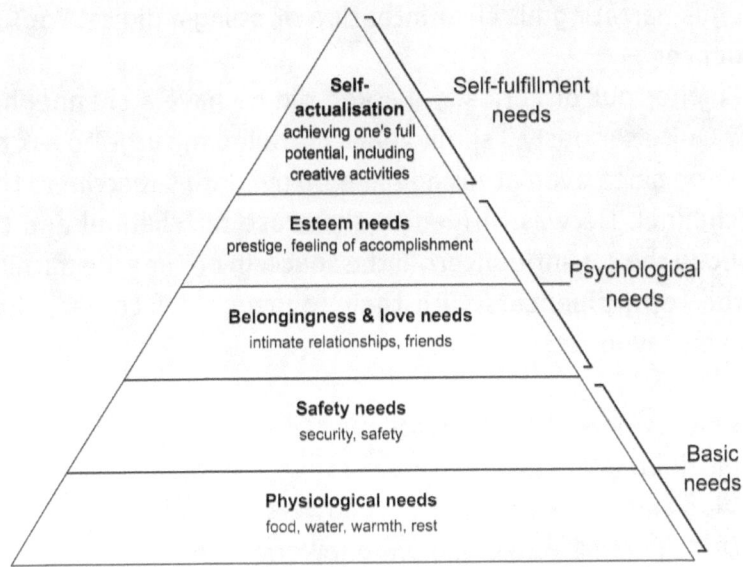

FIGURE 3. MASLOW'S HIERARCHY OF NEEDS
(IMAGE TAKEN FROM WWW.SIMPLYPSYCHOLOGY.ORG).

My Firsthand Not-so-Unusual Experience with Generation Alpha

A while back, I had my friend's young nine-year-old (technically an Alpha) come and visit for dinner. It did not take him much time to break the ice. A very common ice-breaking opening from me (a typical Millennial or Generation Y) is 'What profession do you envision for yourself as you grow older?'

I bet in the not-so-distant past, there would be heroic voices screaming an astronaut, doctor, teacher, engineer. While there was a boy who was looking straight into my eyes and in split seconds narrating his clear intention of being a digital YouTube influencer.

Further out of curiosity, I asked did he have a channel himself? Quite seriously, I should have curtailed my urge to ask this question since even at his age had many more subscribers than my channel. He was thrilled to showcase his channel and talk about all the top influencers in the space. In no time, he narrated all the top influencers with their followers. Of course, these were his favourites:

1. PewDiePie – 110 million followers;
2. Piuzinho – 11.9 million followers;
3. Vlad and Niki – 70.7 million followers;
4. Dude Perfect – 56.6 million followers;
5. Luccas Neto – 35.4 million followers.

This is not an unusual story that you may encounter. It proves the point that career discovery programs are more important than ever before.

From Real-Life Heroes to Digital Heroes

The heroes and inspirations for the younger generations have shifted from real-life champions to digital influencers. While I do not say the digital influencers are not working hard and are less of heroes. I am claiming the idea that the inspirations both positive and negative are only a click away.

A mother exclaims in an interview as mentioned by McCrindle, 'My son never ate cereal, since he did not like it, but because Ryan from YouTube ate it, my son wants to eat the cereal.' Ryan has over twenty-four million subscribers and over thirty-seven billion views of his channel's content. He is barely nine years old. His mother had resigned from her job as a teacher and started to develop the channel full time. Time to think about the pros and cons of such influencers.

Just imagine if you are being mono-focally influenced and your life revolves around one YouTube celebrity. Are you doing justice for the growth of your brain? The question being raised here is what we, as their future stakeholders, can do to prevent such mishaps? It is necessary that we constantly provide resources in real-time that can influence their brains for the better. It is our responsibility to make them understand the subtle nuances of the rapidly changing landscape of work so that they can fit well.

Technological Changes: Curse or Blessing in Disguise?

The technological uproar has presented an undeniable mix of opportunities, benefits, and challenges. Research has consistently shown that the age at which we are exposed to new technology or a transformative event determines how embedded it will become in our psyche and lifestyle.

Children are already learning coding at a very young age in primary school, and are exposed to AI at a much younger age than any other generation before them. Very young children are able to navigate complex digital devices. The benefits should not be offset by the changes in the brain occurring at a lightning speed. A study conducted by the National Institute of Health (NIH) reported that children spending more than two hours of screen per day have demonstrated lower language and thinking test results, and children spending in excess of seven hours per day were found to experience thinning of the brain's cortex. (2)

Is Up-Ageing a Concern?

The entrenched use of media and computers has made this generation grow beyond their age, in a process called 'up-ageing'. Parents and educators have felt the resultant tension. In teaching Generation Alpha, a balance between technological and critical thinking skills has become the need of the hour. It is quite common to see children talking about artificial intelligence and machine learning changing the world of work at a very young age. The common understanding about sex is quite early. The explosive media and the subliminal exposure to the advertisements have made their brains work like toxic junkies. They have more information about the planet Mars than Earth. They have more information about battery-operated cars than bicycles.

The security firm BullGuard surveyed over 2,000 parents of kids aged eight to twelve, and the majority of those parents indicated that they were concerned that their kids were growing up too quickly. Seventy-seven per cent of them blamed the internet for this, and also blamed peer pressure and the increased influence of celebrities in modern culture. (3)

Time to think: By age ten, the majority of the children of parents surveyed owned a cell phone and had a television in their room. Is it a wise move to allow them this privilege?

Equipping Students for an Unknown Future

It is predicted that the next generation is going to have eighteen jobs on average and about six careers spanning their life span — this is way more than any generation in the past. Today the average length of staying in one working role is shortened to under three years. The statistics of the new world of work are mind-boggling. By 2030, it is expected that workers will spend 30% more time learning on the job, 100% more time at work solving problems, 41% more time thinking critically, 77% more time using science and math skills, and 17% of the time using verbal and interpersonal skills. **(4)**

The question that this raises is what kind of cognitive skills our children would need to navigate such changes. Critical thinking, interpersonal skills, science, technology, engineering and mathematics (collectively labelled STEM), and creative thinking, would all be necessary. Can we contribute to the process of the effective development of skills starting early at the high school age rather than waiting for this to occur in college?

To equip children with a lifetime of jobs and careers, we need to make them aware of their potential. What are the future-proofing techniques we need to instil in the new generation?

Generation Alpha: Part of an Unintentional Global Experiment

In no other era has there been significant exposure to screens, a digital explosion, changing economic trends (due partly to the Covid-19 pandemic), and a changing landscape of the job requirements. Due to the flurry of social media platforms like

Snapchat, YouTube, Facebook, TikTok, and Instagram, people are influenced by a network that is connected twenty-four/seven across geographical and social boundaries. Some of the words introduced in the Oxford Dictionary over the last few years include app, cloud, hashtag, selfie, fake news, toxic, lockdown, social distancing, super spreader, and Covid-19.

Undoubtedly so, as exclaimed by the social scientist who coined the term 'Generation Alpha' (McCrindle), this is part of an unintentional global experiment in which digital screens are placed before children at a very early age. The impact on the development of the brain is yet to be studied in detail. Understanding the functioning of children's brains right now is more important than ever before. We really need to be diving deeper, psychologically, into the cognitive functions so that we can better help the children.

The Future-Proofing Technique

The best teachers and parents have always focused on the children first. They have never emphasised *what* they are learning but *how* they are learning and *who* they are becoming in the process. As the world of work changes, the qualities of adaptability, agility, and deep self-discovery will become paramount. Nearly four out of five educators in various research areas agree that creative, people-focused, leadership-oriented and high-level communication skills make the children future-proof as technology will never be able to replace these skills.

We need to focus on developing the cognitive skills of enterprise and innovation on a continuous basis. Transferable skills need to be fostered. The World Economic Forum has come up with the 21st-century skills of lifelong learning in their new vision for education. Figure 4 summarises the skills in detail.

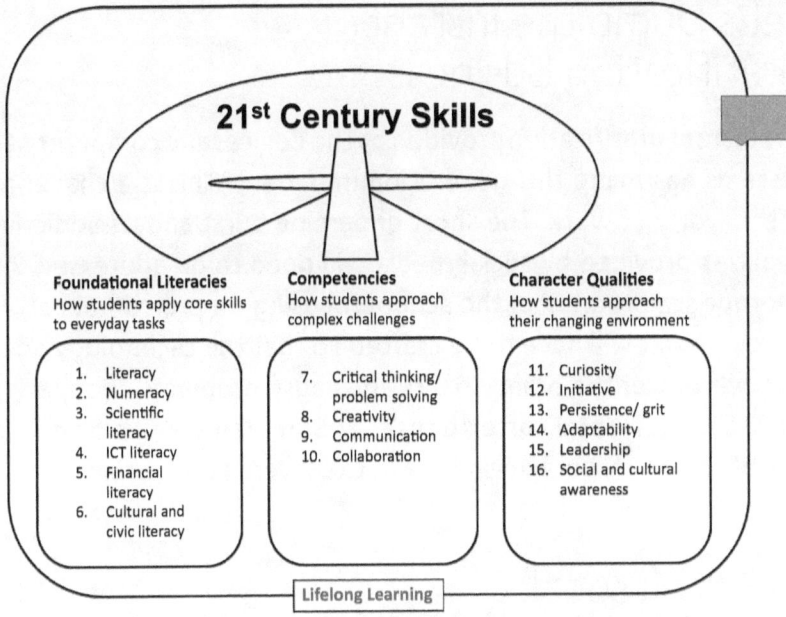

FIGURE 4. DIAGRAM OF 21ST-CENTURY SKILLS (IMAGE COURTESY OF THE WORLD ECONOMIC FORUM).

Claim to Fame

In the era of robotics, automatisation, and computerisation, creativity is what shall be required. Computers are fantastic at doing linear tasks but they are ill-equipped to ideate, function creatively, and innovate. This is the human domain and shall remain the human domain. It is undoubtedly the most feasible claim to fame for the forthcoming generation.

Let's Dump the Instant Gratification Business

The instant gratification provided by the devices and computerised systems has made this generation impatient. This is a challenge in the world of work. The short dopamine burst and its addictive qualities provided by social media will need to be addressed. An appropriate program in the school focusing on prefrontal cortex development will have to be crafted so that the technology does not overpower the brain circuits and cause problems. Wondering what the prefrontal cortex does? Let Sir Ebrall take us on a journey of the brain. Let him showcase the levers of our brain.

Sir Ebrall speaks ...

The Levers in Our Brains

Three of the pathways – the mesocortical, mesolimbic, and nigrostriatal pathways – are considered our 'reward pathways'. They are also the levers. They are responsible for the release of dopamine in various parts of the brain, which shapes the activity of those areas.

Dopamine is a chemical produced by our brains that plays a starring role in motivating behaviour. It gets released when we take a bite of delicious food, when we have sex, after we exercise, and, importantly, when we have successful social interactions.

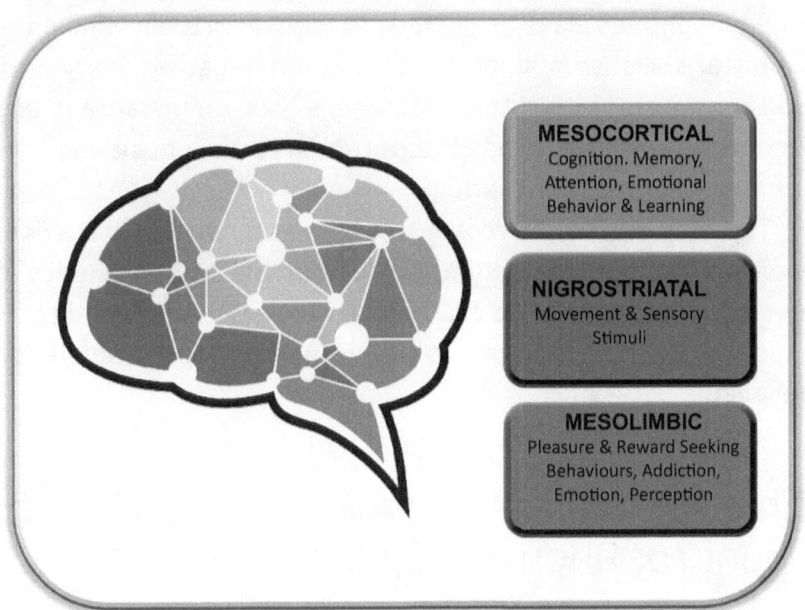

FIGURE 5. CROSS-SECTION OF THE BRAIN SHOWING THE 'REWARD PATHWAYS' (IMAGE BY THE AUTHOR).

While the reward pathways (Figure 5) are distinct in their anatomical organisation, all three become active when anticipating or experiencing rewarding events. In particular, they reinforce the association between a particular stimulus or sequence of behaviours and the feel-good reward that follows. Every time a response to a stimulus results in a reward, these associations become stronger through a process called long-term potentiation.

Although not as intense as a hit of cocaine, positive social stimuli will similarly result in a release of dopamine, reinforcing whatever behaviour preceded it. Cognitive neuroscientists have shown that rewarding social stimuli – laughing faces, positive recognition by our peers, messages from loved ones – activate the same dopaminergic reward pathways.

Smartphones have provided us with a virtually unlimited supply of social stimuli, both positive and negative. Every notification, whether it's a text message, a 'like' on Instagram, or a Facebook notification, has the potential to be a positive social stimulus and dopamine influx.

The only way to overcome this hyper-stimulation behaviour is either through controlling the use of these instruments or media, or to develop the *prefrontal cortex*. Children need to be exposed to the techniques to overcome this hyper-stimulation behaviour.

Time to Ponder – the Average Daily Touch Count for Phones is 2,600 Times

If you've ever misplaced your phone, you may have experienced a mild state of panic until it's been found. In one study, scientists claim that 73% of people experience this unique flavour of anxiety, which makes sense when you consider that adults in the US spend an average of 2–4 hours per day tapping, typing, and swiping on their devices – this adds up to more than 2,600 daily touches. **(5)**

Let's See Now What the Role of the Prefrontal Cortex: Developing the Prefrontal Cortex Essentially Means Winning Over Life

The prefrontal cortex of the brain is the one that is responsible for social control, judgment, discrimination, and executive function. It is this cortex that makes a human, indeed, human. It is not an exaggeration to say that the quality of your life depends on the quality of the decisions you make. Amazingly, the average person makes 35,000 conscious decisions each day. Developing the frontal lobes or the prefrontal cortex of the children by doing focused activities is a must. The frontal cognitive brain circuits need to be fuelled with the right type of creative exercises in the schools and home for them to be developed.

The earlier the children are exposed to techniques like mindfulness, breathing exercises, focus, and concentration, the better that we can develop these circuits. The prefrontal cortex is the most sensitive to parental interaction. The mirror neurons are very strong. Mimicking what the adults are going to do is highly likely. One has to be careful while talking to them. Seeing that you are behaving appropriately in the home is necessary. Exploring simple techniques like super brain yoga, brain button stimulation, brain gym, and mindfulness can all allow children to grow their brain cells. The parenting bond is the key to fixing their prefrontal cortex correctly.

The formula for success for anyone is quite simple, allowing the prefrontal cortex to effectively work without the constant distraction of the limbic (emotional) circuits.

Successful Life = Development of the Executive Function + Critical Thinking 24/7 From Activation of the Prefrontal Cortex Driven Through a Purpose or Meaning

We are all wired with the same formula. This wiring is not going to be altered for many years from now and Generation Alpha will be no different despite the outside changes, the need to contribute, and having a purpose and meaning that is fundamental to human existence is going to remain.

Exercises in Critical Thinking to Develop the Frontal Lobes of the Brain

Generation Alpha is likely to be the most formally educated generation; they will also be the ones who will learn online, upskill across a portfolio of careers, and then redefine the norms of work-life balance. We, as their stakeholders, have dual responsibility for providing them with the right means to explore tomorrow's world of work early on in their early school years and also to support the growth of their innate skills.

The post-school pathway of a career becomes a more prudent discussion than the previous generations as meaningful work and contributions to society will become the dominant ideas nestled in the young minds.

Purpose Over the Pay

Are people happy at work because of the pay that they get? A lovely quote by Prof. Stephen Parker of KPMG brings this home for me: 'Remember, at the end of the day, a good society is one where people are fulfilled, not just prosperous. Higher levels of education do not themselves bring greater job satisfaction, possibly the reverse is the case.'

Time and again in various studies it has been shown that material gain is necessary as an incentive to work but it has never translated into a direct modality to keep one happy. People are happy working when they feel like they are contributing to something, like a common goal or purpose.

Developing Failure Immunity

The fundamental idea is the provision of a safe space for the children to experiment and innovate. The society where failure is condemned has to change. Failure immunity will have to be robustly built. Failure is the raw material of success. Celebrating failures will have to be taught in schools. We will have to overcome the emotional brain's circuits of shame, fear, and pride. We will need to work hard.

Let's Face the Music with Preparation

The world of work of the 21st century will rarely be linear. We will need to be knee-deep in understanding the demands of the time so that we can equip the children with appropriate tools of self-understanding and self-motivation. The forthcoming chapter focuses on preparing for the unknown. It showcases the changing landscape of the world of work. It will also provide insights on how we can be prepared to face the new world.

Walk the Talk

1. How many hours do you spend on your mobile? How often do you monitor your child's screen time? How much green time is available for your child?
2. Narrate your failures that have acted as stepping stones that have actually allowed you to grow and become successful in your career and life.
3. What daily efforts are you taking to see that your children or students grow their prefrontal cortex?

4. Try out super brain yoga and a brain button stimulation exercise. Check out these exercises on www.Mybraindesign®.org

References

1. World Economic Forum. (2020, January). *The Future of Jobs Employment, Skills and Workforce Strategy for the Fourth Industrial Revolution.*
2. Adolescent Brain Cognitive Development study. Read more at https://abcdstudy.org/
3. See the report at https://www.bullguard.com/press/latest-press-releases/2014/14-11
4. World Economic Forum. (2020, October). *The Future of Jobs Report.* https://www.weforum.org/reports/the-future-of-jobs-report-2020/in-full
5. Haynes, T. (2018, May 1). *Dopamine, smartphones & you: A battle for your time.* Harvard BLOG. https://sitn.hms.harvard.edu/flash/2018/dopamine-smartphones-battle-time/

4

The World of Work in the 21st Century: Expect the Unexpected

Diving Deep into the World of Work for Generation Alpha

'The illiterate of 21st century is not the one who cannot read or write, but the one who cannot learn, unlearn, and relearn.'

— ALVIN TOFFLER

How would it feel to travel in a time machine and move forwards to 2050? What would life be like at that time? The future with hyperloop travel, driverless cars, automated humanised robots, a human colony on Mars, properties on the moon, space travel as routine, virtual offices, and fancy AI-based projects is definitely indistinct and far off, but absolutely not inconvincible.

Artificial intelligence, robotics, nanotechnology, genomics, and cryptocurrencies are no longer jargon from progressive thinkers but are shaping our everyday life. The megatrends shaping the world of work are nonlinear. Industry 4.0 is at the cusp of exploding. Industry 4.0 conceptualises rapid change to technology, industries, and societal patterns and processes in the 21st century due to increasing interconnectivity and smart automation.

For students in high school today, the shifts in the workplace will be starker. Generation Alpha's entry into the workforce is just around the corner, and we have to be ready. This chapter focuses on the opportunity awareness for the jobs of tomorrow. It fundamentally shakes the belief that being complacent as educators, teachers, and parents is fine and that time can unfold the skills necessary for the future of work.

Prepare the Dowsing Plans Way Before the Burning Fire

The world today is experiencing the largest shift in the economy since the Industrial Revolution. The workforce has transformed from one dominated by manufacturing, discrete skill requirements, and an expectation of a long tenure in one company, to one that is constantly evolving, expecting a transferable skill set and anticipating changes in jobs.

The latest report on education by Deloitte has said the future could look bleak for two billion young people by the year 2030 unless the global business community shows leadership and comes up with new solutions addressing the skills review and necessary upgrades. (1)

Preparing the next generation with the skills necessary and aligning them towards the future shift could pave a fundamental path of economic prosperity that is even stronger than that achieved by the Millennials. Our job as stakeholders of their future is to provide insights into the world of change, expose Generation Alphas to their real potential, provide the necessary insights about new and emerging careers and guide them into the transition smoothly and confidently.

Think Back in Time

Long before Spotify offered thirty-five million songs to any smartphone, the ability to hear ten full songs wandering away on the road through a Walkman was like the discovery of fire. I bet being a Gen-X myself, this is what I was excited about years back – using a Walkman, a CD player, a pager, a 3kg mobile phone, a trunk call for making international calls and now the sights and sounds of all those fire-driven discoveries have faded.

New Age technology has radically erased those memories. All stakeholders can reminisce exactly the same memories that I am referring to. While we have been witness to all the tragic to magic moments of new technology, we need to be on our game as we guide the younger generations towards their choices for the future world of work.

Our Take on the Generation

While raising the Millennials and Generation Z was no less of a challenge for those Generation X or Baby Boomers, the idea of catching up with the trends was harder then and now even more so. The kids of tomorrow will savour the goals not only of money, prosperity, or power, as was the case in previous generations, but they will also be seeking freedom and happiness.

We have interviewed a lot of parents in Generations X and Y who have their kids going through the career program with us and a common theme of anxiety over the process is being felt. Despite the abundant information available online, this anxiety reflects the gap in understanding the demands of the generation and particularly the lack of insights into the minds of the very young members of Generation Z and Generation Alpha. The incessant debate about robots replacing the world's workforce fosters this fear even further.

Once we are well equipped to know the scientific process of self-discovery, insights into the way the brains of Generation Alphas are shaped, and the world of opportunity of work, we tend to be carefree about career choices.

Our Focus for You and the Children: Are We Prepared?

We will focus on the top shifts that have occurred in careers and jobs over the past decade and also highlight some of the unheard careers of tomorrow that could potentially be hitting the top list over the coming decade. We have done all the hard work for you so that you can save your time experimenting and collecting resources. The summary of the resources is also presented at the end of the chapter.

Jobs and Occupations with Massive Shifts: Robotics are Not Coming; They are Already Here

Certain occupations and job roles will definitely undergo a massive shift. Deloitte has suggested in one of their reports that more than 100,000 jobs in the legal sector have a high chance of being automated in the next twenty years. This is just a unique example, but telemarketing, telesales, manufacturing, dispensing jobs, logistics, other operations, etc., are all potential areas where automation can create significant headway in the near future.

One of the reports suggests that the human share of labour hours will drop from 71% to 58%. Machines and algorithms will increase their contribution by an average of 57%. Regular reports are warning that the automation apocalypse is scary. (2)

Automation Does Not Mean Job Loss

Before we get too deep into the doom and gloom, it is worth stressing that automation isn't synonymous with job losses. Yes, automation is going to happen but ask yourself *are all the jobs at threat*? The answer is clearly no. The reported death of human jobs is an over-exaggeration.

Time has been a testimony to that fact. Technology has, in fact, created more jobs than it has wiped out. This has been called the 'Luddite fallacy', referring back to the 19th-century group of textile workers who smashed the new weaving machinery that made their skills redundant. Automation has really not eliminated any of the single occupations, perhaps with the exception of elevator operators.

Preparing for the Drivers of Change

The fundamental drivers for changes to the world of work are not just technological. Other drivers of change include climate change, the rise of the middle class in emerging markets, aging populations in certain parts of Europe, and the changing aspirations of women.

Short-Term Shock and Long-Term Trends

The Covid-19 viral outbreak with the pandemic-induced lockdowns and global recession of 2020 has paved the way for a highly uncertain outlook for the labour market and the accelerated arrival of the future of work. Automation, in tandem with the global recession, created a double disruption scenario for the world's workforce.

The twin forces of Industry 4.0 and pandemic-induced lockdowns have forced a huge shift towards hybrid workforces, remote working options, e-commerce-driven markets, and vast up-scaling of day-to-day digitalisation.

The 2020 version of the Future of Jobs Survey also reveals similarities across industries when looking at increasingly strategic and increasingly redundant job roles. Similar to the 2018 survey, the leading positions in growing demand are roles such as data analysts and scientists, AI and machine learning specialists, and robotics engineers, all of which are newly emerging among a cohort of roles.

The World Economic Forum's *Jobs of Tomorrow* report, authored in partnership with data scientists at partner companies LinkedIn and Coursera, presented for the first time a way to measure and track the emergence of a set of new jobs across the economy using real-time labour market data. The data from this collaboration identified 99 jobs that are consistently growing in demand across twenty economies. Figure 6 highlights some of these jobs. (3)

Top 20 job roles in increasing and decreasing demand across industries

	Increasing demand		Decreasing demand
1	Data Analysts and Scientists	1	Data Entry Clerks
2	AI and Machine Learning Specialists	2	Administrative and Executive Secretaries
3	Big Data Specialists	3	Accounting, Bookkeeping and Payroll Clerks
4	Digital Marketing and Strategy Specialists	4	Accountants and Auditors
5	Process Automation Specialists	5	Assembly and Factory Workers
6	Business Development Professionals	6	Business Services and Administration Managers
7	Digital Transformation Specialists	7	Client Information and Customer Service Workers
8	Information Security Analysts	8	General and Operations Managers

Increasing demand		Decreasing demand	
9	Software and Application Developers	9	Mechanics and Machinery Repairers
10	Internet of Things Specialists	10	Material – Recording and Stock – Keeping Clerks
11	Project Managers	11	Financial Analysts
12	Business Services and Administration Managers	12	Postal Service Clerks
13	Database and Network Professionals	13	Sales Representative, Wholesale and Manufacturing
14	Robotics Engineers	14	Relationship Managers
15	Strategic Advisors	15	Bank Tellers and Related Clerks
16	Management and Organisation Analysts	16	Door-To-Door Sales, News and Street Vendors
17	FinTech Engineers	17	Electronics and Telecoms Installers and Repairers
18	Mechanics and Machinery Repairers	18	Human Resources Specialists
19	Organisational Development Specialists	19	Training and Development Specialists
20	Risk Management Specialists	20	Construction Labourers

FIGURE 6. JOBS OF TOMORROW LIST (ADAPTED FROM THE WORLD ECONOMIC FORUM 2018 PUBLICATION).

Is the Change Shocking the Brain?

Being a neuroscientist, I always wondered what the newly evolved brain would look like? Probably the best-known model for understanding the history of evolution is the triune brain theory, developed by Paul MacLean. While this theory was quite popular in the 1960s, over the years several elements of this basic model have required revision based on new neuroanatomical discoveries.

Sir Ebrall speaks ...

The three basic brains are shown below (Figures 7 and 8). The three brains do not operate independently but are densely connected through numerous interconnections and have a strong influence on each other. Across seven million years, the human brain has tripled in size, with most of this growth occurring in the past two million years.

3 Brains - Triune Model

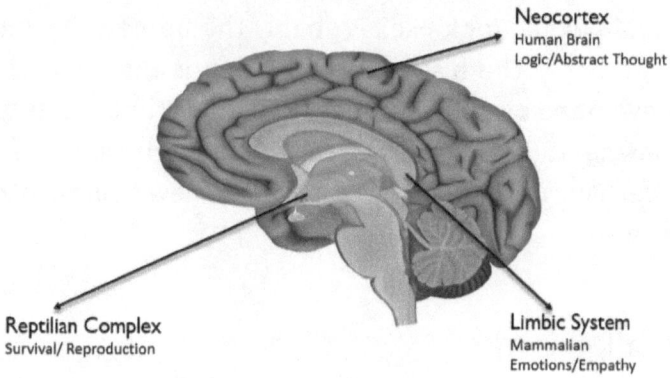

FIGURE 7. IMAGE OF THE TRIUNE BRAIN (IMAGE BY THE AUTHOR)

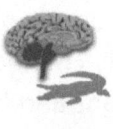
The **reptilian** brain, the oldest of the three, controls the body's vital functions such as heart rate, breathing, body temperature, and balance. The reptilian brain is reliable but tends to be somewhat rigid and compulsive.

The **limbic** brain emerged in the first mammals. It can record memories of behaviours that produced agreeable and disagreeable experience, so it is responsible for what are called emotions in human beings. The main structures of the limbic brain are the hippocampus, amygdala, and hypothalamus.

The **neocortex** first assumed importance in primates and culminated in the human brain with its two large cerebral hemispheres are responsible for the development of human language, abstract thought, imagination, and consciousness.

FIGURE 8. THE THREE 'BRAINS' EXPLAINED (IMAGE BY THE AUTHOR)

The question posed by the scientists is whether the exaggerated use of technology would change the shapes of the brain in any way? Well at this time we do not have a concrete answer to this question.

The Digital Genie is Already Out of the Bottle

We know the digital genie is out of the bottle and is not going anytime soon. The danger paradigm that dominates the current literature on social media and digital technologies is reminiscent of the alarmist rhetoric that had been historically voiced in novels, TV, phones, and the internet. All were feared to erode the moral fabric of the world and lead to the impending doom of civilisation. In the end, none of them turned out to be as bad.

There are downsides to the current digital explosion and the Industry 4.0 revolution. However, there is an imminent upside as well, particularly the focus on school children and building their skills for tomorrow which allows us to lessen the gloom.

There is a Significant Upside to Technology

The way globalisation is shunning the boundaries between the countries of the world is just unbelievable. The pace of collaboration and the outcomes from these far-ended partnerships from one part of the world to the other are no less than magic.

A few years back, after completing my MBA from Cambridge University, I was doing a project with the UNNCD at the United Nations Institute for Training and Research (UNITAR). Our team was working in five different time zones and thanks to the digitalisation and the available media to connect, we could do the work well beyond efficiency. It was a mammoth task of launching a program for non-communicable diseases in over ninety countries.

Our Immediate Focus for Children

Allowing the human brain of tomorrow to focus on more creativity, self-inquiry, soft (interpersonal) skills, developing lasting relationships, working for advancing the human race, and unearthing the mysteries of the supreme consciousness would form the miraculous escape from the downsides proposed from the technological revolution.

It is important and necessary to pay attention to the changing skills landscape. It is our duty to focus on the skills of our children and have programs to expose the children to these new technological landscapes. This is particularly relevant to the Asian context. The children are still being taught the old curriculum and teachers have not adapted themselves to the latest developments.

What Can We Do as Parents and Teachers?

We need to equip ourselves sufficiently and up-level our understanding of the relevant shifts and changed roles so that we can explore these at the right pace with the children and slowly induct them into the realities of the new digital world. We must be able to support them through the transition. Starting a dialogue early in high school is a must.

We need the schools to build an expanded curriculum showcasing the demands of tomorrow so that the children's young brains are primed to anticipate even the unexpected. Parents have even bigger roles to play. Having the time to be involved in the decisions of their children and discussions about the future is important.

Leaving the Career Decision to a Child is offering an AK-47 Gun to a Drunkard

Leaving young children to career discovery on their own is not ideal since the half-developed frontal lobe of the children is not serving them to make the right decision. Yes, the decision has to be done bilaterally without enforcing our thoughts and ideas, but leaving the decision to them is like offering an AK-47 to a drunkard. Okay, this is an exaggerated analogy, but I want to reinforce the idea vividly since I have seen parents from America, India, Japan and Canada speaking the same language.

I am quite worried when I hear those statements. My point of view is straight from neuroscience and until the time the frontal lobes are not myelinated (the brain cover over the brain cell or neuron is called myelin), expecting teenagers to be confident in their own decisions is a far-fetched fantasy. You know about this from the last chapter.

Where Can We Start?

We should start from the point of acquiring knowledge about the shifts and changes in the world of work. We need to understand the skills that will be required for tomorrow. We then need to focus on the new and so far unheard of roles and learn about those. A few proposed career groups are presented here, which may become the norm for tomorrow. **(4)**

1. Virtual store Sherpa: Will focus on customer satisfaction through virtually advising customers using the knowledge of the product line.

2. Personal data broker: Will ensure consumers receive revenue from their data.
3. Personal memory curator: Will consult with patients to generate specifications for virtual reality experiences.
4. Augmented-reality journey builder: Will collaborate with talented engineers and technical artists to develop vital elements for clients.
5. Body-part maker: Will create living body parts for athletes, soldiers, and others who lose parts of the anatomy.
6. Nano-medic: Will transform healthcare by providing a completely new industry paradigm.
7. Genetic modifier or recombinant farmer: Will transform farming and livestock in automated and smart ways.
8. Elderly wellness consultant: Will cater to the physical and mental needs of the elderly.
9. Memory augmentation doctors: Will boost patients' memory when it hits capacity by allowing insertion of the chip to advance the memory.

You may be wondering if all this is some science fiction story. Well, I thought so too until I went through the report. An indication of these imminent roles by 2030 is clear. According to the McKinsey Global Institute's research report (5), the top three skill sets the workers will need to secure the best careers will be higher cognitive abilities, social and emotional abilities, and technological skills.

Would University Degrees be Obsolete?

Well, the question has been posed to multiple educational experts over the last few years and a consistent verdict or direction is yet to arrive. But looking into the changes spanning the various industries of travel, communications, and health, there is no doubt that a radical change in the field of university education is coming.

We have a flurry of tools allowing us to learn stuff at our desired time and place. There are platforms like YouTube, Coursera, Udemy, TED, and Udacity that are slowly decentralising the power of disbursement of education from the universities. The quality of education is improving every single day. The teachers who were struggling to find jobs are now teaching across boundaries. The tools required to develop courses are becoming cheaper and more widely available.

Well, the traditional libraries are almost becoming extinct. The administrators of the various universities are well aware that a few of the degree courses are actually redundant and have no practical value in helping the students get appropriate jobs.

The University Education Offered as an *À La Carte*

We are not far from where the entrepreneurs of today will revolutionise the future of education of tomorrow. Steve Jobs disrupted the music industry years ago when he changed the way we bought singles instead of buying albums. The future students will be able to choose between hundreds of subjects and assemble their own personalised career certificates. There will no longer be a 'typical' university endorsing those degrees or courses.

Could Interviews for Jobs Become Obsolete?

Interviews may not remain the ideal way to find the best person for the job. Interviews in the future may look nothing like what they do today. Personality profiling may be the thing of tomorrow. This may be done through the help of AI or social media information. Credit scores for skills, job performance tests being done virtually, wearable health technology indicating the candidate's health-brain set and showcasing their ability to do the job, and a portfolio of jobs or careers rather than a few skills will likely become central to the job selection process in the future.

Machine learning-driven selection of the right candidates through matching of advanced skills, digital personas, and digital reputation would all be considered for the right selection of the candidates. Our job is to expose the children to these technologies right from early high school. Providing information through the media is not enough. The brain clearly learns by doing.

Sir Ebrall's tip ...

Learning by Doing

Learning by doing refers to a theory of education proposed by John Dewey. It's a hands-on approach to learning, meaning students must interact with their environment in order to adapt and learn. (6)

'I believe that the school must represent present life-life as real and vital to the child as that which he carries on in the home, in the neighbourhood, or on the playground.' –John Dewey (*My Pedagogic Creed*)

From a neurological perspective, we see that learning happens as a result of the brain's response to positive and negative feedback encountered while performing a task. Imagine a child hitting a ball for the first time. When the bat connects with the ball, the child's brain is flooded with dopamine and all the neurotransmitters that are a crucial element of our reward system. The activation of the reward system maximises the likelihood that the child will be able to hit the ball a second time. In contrast, if the child misses the ball, her error-correction system will activate, and the child will adjust her swing accordingly. This release of neurotransmitters encourages us to adapt our behaviour in order to avoid errors.

In high school education, many studies have shown that experiential learning achieves the consolidation of memory, which other methods cannot reinforce. Learning by doing makes the brain pathways strong. The chemicals are relayed efficiently and neuronal growth is amplified.

Catching the Wave: The 21st-Century Career

Surfing can be scary even on the brightest of days. When children's futures are at stake, career surfing can feel treacherous especially as the waves can cast them off guard as new waves of technology keep rising.

While the students will have to learn to thrive and navigate in this new world of careers, we have a huge responsibility in preparing them to expect the anticipated changes. We need to be prepared to be able to apply the career discovery process appropriately for our kids. The idea of this book is to provide these tools and processes that have been validated.

The pyramid of career success allows the child to strengthen each level of career success. The idea of the *Mybraindesign*® program is not merely to provide a personality insight or cognitive thinking style, but to promote information relay of more than 800 careers to the young brains. The idea is to catch the wave of the 21st century by learning to career surf.

Being Aware, Care and Dare

A very eloquent quote by my spiritual teacher many years ago was 'Being aware, you care and then you dare'. The necessary next steps are understanding the futuristic megatrends and aligning the current skills and cognitive patterns of the child with the prescription of the necessary skills so that the transition is picture-perfect.

It is All Well in the End

This chapter has provided a lot of hope and hype. Being prepared for tomorrow is a no-brainer. Again, finding the right career path is no mathematical formula. There are no tests or counsellors who can be meticulous fortune tellers. There is no fixed method to showcase a firm answer. But there is a process that can make all the anxieties and fears take a back seat. This is the idea behind crafting the pyramid formula.

The Process is not Complex Nor is the Science Behind the Formula

Well, you must be wondering: *What is that process and how can you be hands-on in the process?* You must have been following various tools, methods, and processes for career discovery in your school or home. So you must be asking yourself why you need one more neuroscience-based approach. Let us first see the trends of career discovery and talk further about the pyramid of career success and *Mybraindesign®*.

Walk the Talk

1. Narrate some more of the weird jobs of tomorrow in addition to those mentioned in the chapter.
2. Now that you know the three brains, describe an amygdala hijack? Hint: You may need Google support.
3. Look around for robots and automation. How many job types are taken over by these factors? E.g., Tally has made my accountant redundant, the chatbot has replaced the real talking guy and the registration robot has surpassed the need for a receptionist in my hospital.

References

1. See Deloitte 2030 jobs prediction press release at www.gbc-education.org
2. World Economic Forum. (2018, September). *The Future of Jobs Report.* https://www.weforum.org/reports/the-future-of-jobs-report-2018
3. World Economic Forum. (2020, October). *The Future of Jobs Report.* https://www.weforum.org/reports/the-future-of-jobs-report-2020/in-full
4. Cognizant and Zdnet research on the jobs of tomorrow 2030.
5. Dondi, M., Klier, J., Panier., F. & Schubert, J. (2021, June 25) *Defining the skills citizens will need in the future world of work.* McKinsey & Company. https://www.mckinsey.com/industries/public-and-social-sector/our-insights/defining-the-skills-citizens-will-need-in-the-future-world-of-work
6. Study.com. (2018, March 23). *John Dewey on education: Impact & theory.* https://study.com/academy/lesson/john-dewey-on-education-impact-theory.html

5
Is There a Perfect Career Tool?

Narrowing Wide Career Choices to the One Perfect Choice is Both an Art and Science

'A career is not just about earning an income. It is about pursuing the essence of your life.'

— TERRY MANTE

There is no doubt that making the right choice is a daunting task. There are currently about 12,000 career options, including vocational work, in the world. Even developing countries like India have about 250 careers in more than forty industries with some 40,000 individual job titles. In North America, there are even more job options and career choices; more choices can mean more confusion.

Everyone talks about choosing the right career and doing the job that you are great at, but no one really tells you how to do this exactly. A lot of career advisers give personality tests and various other tests with the intent to discover the best career choices for students. Some suggest actually taking a gap year and figuring out one's real calling. Some quizzes and sites are meant to provide career choices through an automated algorithm. There are plentiful online tests, most of which are available for free.

It is impossible to have a single snapshot of the complex functioning of the brain function and hence no personality test or other psychometric test can potentially be picture-perfect for the decision. The question then arises: *How can we best predict which career is ideal for a student right from the start?*

We all know human nature is dynamic. Can a single assessment cater to these dynamics? No! None of the methods has proven to predict what one can or will choose well ahead of time. Utilising career tests on their own is not the right way forward. The career assessment methods have limitations.

The results are only as valid as the input. Test takers may unknowingly answer questions inaccurately. High school students or young adults may answer questions based on what their parents want or based on how they think they should answer.

What is an Ideal Career Evaluation Process?

The ideal career evaluation process is aimed to answer the following questions that take the teacher or parent through a series of steps:

1. Helping to plan and prepare for the most ideally suitable career;
2. Helping the child perform a self-SWOT (strengths, weaknesses, opportunities and threats);
3. Helping to understand the child's way of thinking;
4. Aligning the interests of the children to their career goals;
5. Providing tools for overcoming any resistance or obstacles along the proposed path;
6. Coming to understand the various career and jobs, particularly of the 21st century;
7. Allowing a hands-on understanding of the various job roles;
8. Understanding the demand-supply projection for each career;
9. Providing opportunities for skill-building aligning to career goals from early high school.

In this chapter, we shall delve into the concepts of self-discovery and its importance. We shall also be reviewing some commonly used methods and techniques for evaluation by career counsellors worldwide.

Nostalgic Moments to Savour

Let us look back a few decades back when we were choosing careers for ourselves. I vividly remember the options in front of me. There were only two choices because I was a science student: engineering or medicine. I remember my mother and me going pillar to post trying to seek the answer from others for the right career path. I remember going to teachers, colleagues of my father, colleagues' parents, and peers.

And each person would be offering advice from his or her own perspective and opportunity awareness that he or she possessed. This reality still holds true after two decades. While the era has completely changed, the confusion remains the same. More choices have led to more confusion. I was very lucky that, finally, my career went the best way. But not all can be lucky.

One of the surveys in Canada suggested that three-quarters of Canadian workers who had seen a career coach wished that they had chosen a different career. The survey included more than 1,350 professionals in various fields.

Is this not mind-boggling?

A Resonating Analogy

Let us compare the whole discovery of the right career choice to a game of golf. The last hole is our destination – the ideal career choice. Let us assume the green patch is the right path to reach the hole. The sand and other rough areas are the detours that hope to avoid. The idea of the career assessment methodology is to land on the green patches and avoid the rough patches. The final navigation to the end hole for a great career choice in life would be easier once you land on the green patch.

A career assessment is a scientific tool that helps the counsellor and the students to identify potential career choices. They are often based on one of the psychometric assessments built by psychologists. Some tests are one-offs while some have to be repeated based on age. Most of the tests target personality, aptitude, and interests in varying combinations. Many such tests are available for free online. Some tests do not need physical counselling while most need it. The interpretation of the tests is also key.

These assessments usually have multiple choice questions and are designed by psychologists. They are structured in a way that in the end, you get to know the range of careers that align with your parametric evaluation.

My Personal Insights

I have personally performed more than seventy-two career assessment tests and have developed a keen interest in testing them for my students and checking out their reliability. While the statistics may differ here and there, the idea for me is to reinforce to parents and teachers that relying solely on the findings without taking into consideration other factors like social background, career values, financial obligations of the family, personal choices, and interests, peer pressure, and other available options in the school or city, one cannot confidently develop a career plan.

The Four Pillars of Success

The four important pillars for a successful investment in the career discovery process are- understanding the career assessment methodology, discussing the accuracy of the results of the assessment, the career coach structured interview, and most importantly, the alignment of various other factors aiding in the choice of the right career. Accuracy and reliability are tested based on statistical models, sampling, and methodology used.

Used wisely, career assessments can help you acquire a better sense of the types of jobs and activities that might be a good fit for you. Too often, however, people who take career tests misunderstand them, misuse them (almost always unintentionally) or mistake them for being more reliable than they really are.

The sheer number of options along with the new-age careers have even challenged various personalities and interests' inventories. The neuroscience suggesting that brains are plastic has also challenged the notion that a brain consolidates at a certain age.

Career Tests Aren't 'Tests' at All

The word 'test' implies right or wrong answers, but most career assessments don't have right and wrong answers. Whatever career assessments you choose to pursue, it is important to know before starting that your goal isn't to be right, but to be accurate and true to yourself.

Career Assessments Suggest: They Don't Tell

No matter which career test you take, its purpose isn't to tell you a specific career to pursue. No tool is that powerful. All a career assessment can do is suggest ideas about careers you might want to explore in more depth.

Think about it this way: If any career test could accurately tell you which occupation to go into, wouldn't everyone be taking it? Wouldn't you be paying a hefty sum to avoid the hassles of career experience later? Wouldn't everyone be happy and satisfied in their jobs?

Garbage In Equals Garbage Out: The GIGO Principle is True in This Context Too

A career test's results will only be as good as the information you offer in your responses. Being honest is the key.

Consider Your Results With a Very Open Mind

I have personally seen students and teachers laughing off the suggestions arising from the tests. Don't make such tragic errors. Thoroughly explore the suggestions showing up on the tests. Remember, we often confirm inherently to the bias of choosing what we already know.

Some career assessments – like, for instance, the Strong Interest Inventory® – offer a list of potential careers that might be a good match. I like to review all the assessments done for the child before I even let the child perform our self-discovery process. Our assessment relies more on the neurodevelopmental concepts and is unlike the interest inventory or other commonly used personality instruments.

Reading Between the Lines of Your Results

For most of the tests that I performed online or offline, entrepreneurship was always one of the recommendations. While, initially, I was not aware that I had this hidden fire of entrepreneurship in me, repeated showcasing of this career choice finally led me to observe my tendencies. Indeed, I was then able to recognise my implicit and inherent interests in creation. Entrepreneurship is nothing but taking creativity to the masses, keeping profit and purpose in mind.

Beware of Junk

There are many career 'tests' available online. Some of these tools are quite reliable and valid, but many are not. Explore career assessments with a dose of scepticism. Never be fooled by the bells and whistles as presented on the website. The reviews are easy to generate from a paid media agency. Speak to real people. Has the test you're about to take, and perhaps pay good money for, been well-researched so it accurately measures what it claims to measure?

I am a deep critic and will not accept any test without reading the dedicated literature showcasing its construct validity or face validity and test-retest reliability. Simply put, it should measure what it is supposed to measure, and it should be replicable when tested again in other circumstances.

The test should not be influenced by mood, circumstances, intelligence, etc. It should portray the personality factors. I am personally not a great fan of the Myers–Briggs Type Indicator. Over two million people take it annually. However, using the test for determining career options or as a pre-employment survey, fails to understand its true essence.

What is MBTI?

Captivated by Jung's ideas, the mother-daughter team of Katharine Briggs and Isabel Myers published the Myers–Briggs

Type Indicator (MBTI®) questionnaire in 1943. There are sixteen personality subtypes of the MBTI. The various combinations of the letters then help in determining the personality type. Various career inventories across the globe utilise either of the above as their base.

The test claims that based on ninety-three questions, it can group all the people of the world into sixteen different discrete 'types' – and in doing so, serve to be 'a powerful framework for building better relationships, driving positive change, harnessing innovation, and achieving excellence'. But the test was developed in the 1940s based on the totally untested theories of Carl Jung and is now thoroughly disregarded by the psychology community. Even Jung warned that his personality 'types' were just rough tendencies he'd observed, rather than strict classifications.

Many researchers and analysts have shown the test is totally ineffective at predicting people's success in various jobs, and that about half of the people who take it twice get different results each time. While I personally had the same experience of having two distinct personality types at two different times in my life.

Don't Get Test-Happy

You can easily convince yourself that you're doing something about your career concerns by completing some career assessments. But it's easy to fall into the trap of doing so much testing that you're not taking any other constructive action in your career focus. Career choice is not merely relying on the evaluation of the tests. The actions stemming from the tests are the main next go-to task.

This is the reason our career methodology and philosophy are not limited to an assessment. It should be all-encompassing.

The Paralysis-by-Analysis

Go easy on the number of tests you complete. There are lots of other things you can and should be doing to explore your career options, like informational interviewing or reading books about a field of potential interest. Too many options raised from the tests could also mean that one is unable to decide.

Career assessments have helped many thousands of people get a better sense of where they might fit in the world of work. But thousands of other people who have taken career tests would have been much better off not using them at all.

No Ideal Time to Do the Tests: Only Ideal Method

Students and parents often ask 'When is the right time to take the career assessment?' Well, the question should be framed instead as 'What methodology can one use for a particular age to help understand career choices?' Change is constant in nature and our skills and aptitudes *do* change over time.

In case you are going for a methodology that does not evaluate any of the above, it is fine to have a one-shot test after the eighth grade (twelve to thirteen-year-olds).

Some inventories that focus on interests and other particular aptitude tests may need repeat testing depending on one's age. Prior to the eighth grade, often students lack the ability to fully self-conceptualise and hence it is not advisable to perform a psychometric test. Having a structured process and not a one-time assessment is the key to successful career discovery.

Subjects and Curriculum Choices: Resolving a Complex Dilemma

In certain countries, the choice of curriculum and subjects also becomes an important step. The Cambridge Advanced course is well known for its flexibility. Schools have a choice of fifty-five subjects and the freedom to offer them in almost any combination.

Learners can specialise in or study a broad range of subjects. It becomes prudent to choose the right subjects that further can be built into the career college option. Acquiring an insight early on in the process of career choice allows the student to better understand the concepts.

Fundamentals First: What is a Psychometric Assessment?

A psychometric assessment is a scientific way to identify the existing skills and interests of students to assess their personalities. Psychometric is derived from the word 'psyche', which means mind, and metrics mean measurement. Criteria for a psychometric test are reliability and validity. However, the student must attempt the test honestly and provide spontaneous answers.

Often the children try to answer the questions so that it fits the norm. They are often afraid of being judged as they answer the so-called tests. The assessments should not be limited but all expansive. The ideal time for appearing for an interest and aptitude test is in eighth grade (twelve to thirteen-year-olds).

By and large, the brain is fully developed in terms of cognitive preferences by the age of thirteen years. We have confidently tested statistically our self-discovery tool and it works just perfect from the age of thirteen.

Some Commonly Opted Assessments

The various personality tests and aptitude tests used around the world have their basis in either the Holland hexagonal theory (also called RIASEC, see below) or the Myers–Briggs personality test.

The Holland Inventory is one of the most frequently found online career interest tools available. It includes six interest themes/domains described by John Holland in relation to the Strong Interest Inventory. These are the Realistic (R), Investigative (I), Artistic (A), Social (S), Enterprising (E), and Conventional (C) domains – collectively known as RIASEC (Figure 9). This, and the Myers–Briggs personality test, are often used in combination.

Holland's theory rests on four basic assumptions that describe how occupational interests are developed. The first assumption states that individuals can be categorised into RAISEC types stated above. The second assumption asserts that environments (e.g., places of employment) are also categorised into the same six types. The third assumption is that individuals tend to choose environments that fit their personalities. And the fourth assumption highlights the importance of one's personality being congruent with his or her environment. It states that behaviour is determined by the fit between an individual's personality and the environment in which he or she is surrounded.

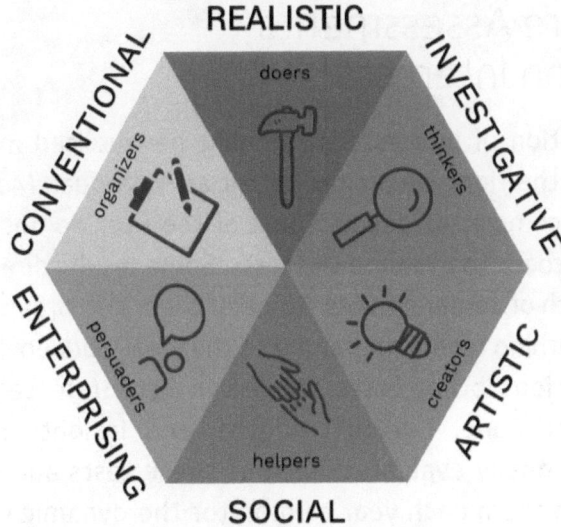

FIGURE 9. HOLLANDS'S MODEL (ADAPTED FROM SMART, J. C., FELDMAN, K. A., & ETHINGTON, C. A. (2000). *ACADEMIC DISCIPLINES: HOLLAND'S THEORY AND THE STUDY OF COLLEGE STUDENTS AND FACULTY.* VANDERBILT UNIVERSITY PRESS.)

What are Aptitude Tests?

Aptitude assessments are also utilised as one of the core assessments of the evaluation methods. The aptitude tests are again multiple-choice questions throwing light on the ability to perform a certain set of cognitive tasks appropriately. It can involve the determination of the various facets of spatial visualisation, numerical reasoning, linguistic ability, mechanical potential, perceptual speed, creativity, etc.

What are Assessments Based on Interests?

The evaluation of interests is the next best-utilised method for evaluating the right career choice for an individual. Most assessments are completely online. Some of the sites do not provide a mentor or coach to evaluate the tests. Some results directly showcase a bunch of career choices. Some of them also provide insights into the learning techniques and also the ideal work environment.

The various other tests applied in corporate settings are DiSC, Color Code, CliftonStrengths, and Insights Discovery. I have personally evaluated each of these tests and make it a habit to do them each year to monitor the dynamic evaluation of the various tests pertaining to my personal cognitive growth.

Are These Tests Valid in the Post-modern Context of the 21st Century?

One must remember that these tests were developed in the 20th century. RIASEC was designed to address the vocational issues of people living in the United States. Although Holland's system has been subjected to more empirical tests than any other vocational theory, it still remains in the early phases of cross-cultural research. (1) Some scholars argue that the post-modern world renders most established vocational theories irrelevant in a world marked by rapid change. (2)

Enough research has shown that the brain is plastic and that experiences continue to shape our personalities and the way we interact with the world every single day. It is important for the test not to pigeonhole a student into a specific set of choices. Understanding the process is the key.

The assessment on which I worked for many years was a derivative of Neethling Brain Instrument (NBI) and Herrmann Brain Dominance Instrument (HBDI). I used to test every year to see if there was a significant change in my analysis. While both assessments have fantastic reliability, I never found any major change in the results even when tested at varied times. However, many other personality tests and aptitudes have shown different results at different points in time.

The Final Dictum 'Know Thyself' Applies to Every Area of Our Life Experience

I am convinced that no assessment tool is perfect. The complete process is the key. Reading between the lines is a must. Being a counsellor to thousands of students, I am convinced that allowing the child to take the results to the next level of understanding is a must. Relying on an open-ended neurodevelopmental tool can help the child to identify the strengths and opportunities and allow him or her to work on the skills so that the best career choices can be determined for the individual and also that the overall development of the brain is ideal.

Constructive skill-building, hobby crafting, and potential career choices can be provided even at an early age in high school using the right self-discovery methods.

Remember Also That Career is Again Just One Part of Life

There is no doubt that career discovery is an important part of life. But life has to be lived with conscious awareness about the self and one's surroundings. The exercises allow the children to be exposed to the way they behave and think, allowing them to relate to the world much better.

We already saw that the future world of work will be unique and challenging. There are more avenues than ever before, creating a mass of confusion. To allow children to try and test a career may work provided we are primed by our inner strengths and aware of our potential blind spots.

Science Never Fails to Help but Being Aware is the Key

We, as the guardians of Generation Alpha, have to improve our knowledge and understanding of the various AI-based tools and other sophisticated personality evaluations relevant to this era so that we can empower the children to embrace success with ease. There is no doubt that science never fails to help. It is just that being aware of the pitfalls and values clearly is required so that we do not overemphasise the choices provided by the tools nor do we underestimate their value.

Success is Nothing But Constant Reskilling and Upskilling the Self

Life is an ongoing stream of experiences and using the science of self-discovery appropriately and at the right juncture in life for the students helps them make informed decisions about their career choices. Success is nothing but adopting and constantly reskilling and upskilling ourselves. The measures of success are often different for different people. The external measures of success are money, stability, comfort, and praise while the internal measures are satisfaction, self-confidence, fulfilment, and finding a meaning or purpose for life.

I would have never pursued an MBA from Cambridge University after having a successful career as a neurologist if I had ever comfortably accepted the external criteria for success. Relooking at the final career goal posts multiple times and starting right from high school is important and necessary.

Our consistent hard work for a decade has led us to build a pyramid of career success. In the next chapter, we shall review the method in detail. I am confident that the insights provided about self-discovery science shall go a long way in confirming its role in career and life choices for all of us.

Walk the Talk

1. Narrate all the assessments that you have been performing for your children. Check the basic methodology and check its outcomes.
2. **Nostalgeering**: We did some visioneering for the future. Let us go back in time for each of our career journeys and design three other proposed futures for us.
3. Let us check your short-term memory. Narrate the elements required for a perfect or ideal career assessment. Remember, the only way to gain control over the memory is to repeat and revise. You can read the elements again and come back to jot the same.

References

1. Spokane, A. R., & Cruza-Guet, M. C. (2005). Holland's theory of vocational personalities in work environments. In S. D. Brown and R. W. Lent (Eds.), *Career development and counseling: Putting theory and research to work* (pp. 24–41). Wiley.
2. Savickas, M. L., Nota, L., Rossier, J., Dauwalder, J.-P., Duarte, M. E., Guichard, J., Soresi, S., Van Esbroeck, R. & van Vianen, A. E. M. (2009). Life designing: A paradigm for career construction in the 21st century. *Journal of Vocational Behaviour, 75*(3), 239–250.

6

What *is* the Difference in the Difference?

The Validated, Neuroscience-based Process of Career Discovery is the Key to Our Method

'The best way to predict the future is to create it.'

— ABRAHAM LINCOLN

Have you ever wondered what the average human life span is in hours? It is essentially 750,000 hours. If we subtract the hours spent as a child and also the time we spend sleeping and completing other daily chores, we are left with 250,000 hours of meaningful work. The interesting thing about these sums is that they boil down to the point that the majority of hours in our lives are spent working a career or job.

A job should not be equated to a career. Jobs can be many while a career may be one or many. This indicates the necessity to choose the right path which is fulfilling and satisfying.

Research has shown that humans are remarkably bad at predicting how they feel when doing something in the future. Choosing the right career path is one of the most confusing and anxiety-riddled experiences not just for high school students, but even for some students following graduation. Following your heart or doing what you love are highly overrated statements for a high school student.

The idea of this book is to help facilitate the use of the scientific tool for this discovery process. While predicting happiness for the future is not possible, predicting choices that are based on the mental make-up of the child through the *Mybraindesign*® evaluation is definitely possible.

We already discussed various self-discovery tools in the last chapter. In this chapter, we shall focus on our technique for identifying the best career choices that are built with years of experience and scientific validation.

How to think is More Important Than *What* to Think

Each person is born with specific thinking potential. He or she possesses a unique pattern of thinking. It is not important for us to gauge what our children are thinking so much as *how* they are thinking. Once we can understand the wiring pattern of the brain, we can provide them with relevant career options and also allow them to take appropriate steps in the direction of a particular career.

They can also understand the pitfalls in their thinking potential, which allows them to learn and relearn the missing patterns. Beyond accuracy or reliability, I believe the beauty of any tool is the potential to provide an insight into tapping the unknown or hidden potentials.

The Seven-Step Career Success Pyramid

We discussed the seven-step formula for career success in the previous chapter. Let us now deep dive into it. My team and I have spent years determining the world of work that will occur in the near future and equating the same to the thinking patterns and designs for the individual.

The idea for me was always to provide a career discovery process that is as robust as possible.

The pyramid of career discovery success identifies seven important steps in the career journey.

1. **Self-discovery**: The first prime step performed through *Mybraindesign®*, a proprietary test algorithm based on artificial intelligence and whole-brain science.
2. **Opportunity awareness**: Brainforia's career quest allows students to gain exposure to more than 800 careers through a dedicated hands-on activity-based program.
3. **Career consciousness focus**: Sustained and focused attention on a select group of careers. The top five-star careers in the *careerpik* module through the career cluster maps.

4. *Lifedesign blueprint*®: A summary of the internal and external factors influencing the career choice (to be discussed in the forthcoming chapter).
5. **Upskilling by flow and grow:** A skill-gap inventory and hobby crafting idea map allowing the child to build the necessary skills and hobbies in their early high school years based on the dominant and non-dominant thinking types defined as core and satellite skills.
6. **Success signatures:** Understanding the various ingredients of the personality types having successful careers. Modelling the real-life heroes.
7. **Career choice success:** The celebration of a successful life

I wish that the schools adopted the pyramid of career success discovery as a curriculum rather than a one-off snapshot evaluation. As mentioned in previous chapters, my research team and I have utilised advanced AI and career satisfaction data of thousands of students through prospective analysis and whole-brain science to build the formula.

The relatively short-sounding seven-point journey for any student has been developed through years of hard work. The same pyramid is applicable for an adult who is stuck in his or her career or a college-going student failing to understand the next best step. The basic formula is no different. It's just that the options are more tuned to suit the end goal.

FIGURE 10. THE PYRAMID OF CAREER CHOICE (DIAGRAM BY THE AUTHOR).

Rome Was Not Built in a Day

Each of the levels of the pyramid (Figure 10) in the discovery process is well researched and considered. The pyramid was built to encompass all the ingredients required to take the best and next career move be it for high school students or college-going students. The idea was to empower the stakeholders in helping the future generation.

I started my research on the science of career choice in early 2000. My own career progression and success were on experimental grounds. I could never have done what I did in my life if I was not consciously aware of each step of a vision for myself and the motivation for success.

Let's Think About Some Fundamental Questions

What are we essentially looking out for our children and their future? Are we chasing success for them? Is money the end goal? What makes us look into the decision of career choice so seriously? The answer is very clear. We spend the majority of our lives performing work-related tasks. Hence, doing the right type of work suitable to our cognitive make-up is essential.

Our world of work has a direct influence on our relationships, health, and happiness. Time and again, the world happiness report has stressed that people who are satisfied and happy in their work are the ones who have a happy work life.

Connecting the Dots Forwards for the Kids is Important

Most of us as adults realise the dots of career and life connect backwards while it is important that we connect the dots for our children forward. Children are the partners in this journey of discovery. Dictating our choices or believing their choices is not right. Of course, they should be the torchbearers of the whole process.

The First Step is the Building Block for Career Success: Self-Discovery Insights

The first and crucial step of self-discovery is the *Mybraindesign*® assessment. *Mybraindesign*® is a self-discovery tool with more than thirty-five questions built to know the thinking style of the child. It is a simple assessment requiring no fancy skills. It is highly reproducible and is proven to be reliable.

The assessment is offered online in the comfort of the child's home. All instructions are made clear to them. It is important that they answer the questions honestly. There are no right or wrong answers. The assessment is merely highlighting the preferences in chronological order of best to least. The assessment does not take more than thirty minutes.

Thinking is Like a Genie

Thinking is like a genie of the brain allowing the brain to perform any task by merely pushing a button. Thinking only prompts action. Understanding thinking is crucial. *Mybraindesign*® is a mirror of our thinking preferences laid out in the two-by-four model.

Of further interest is that the chronology of the preferences can be extrapolated to build seventeen different design patterns of thinking. Each of the designs pertains to a particular career cluster. Let us see the magic unfold in the forthcoming chapter.

Opportunity Awareness Gap

A shocking survey published a few years back in India indicated a staggering 93% of students between fourteen and twenty-one are aware only of about seven potential career options. (1) Our own study of more than 500 students has revalidated these findings and the maximum number of careers the children were aware of never exceeded ten.

You may be wondering at this stage how they could not be aware with so much social media and Google exposure. Without motivation and a will to know the meaning behind the search, children are never going to voluntarily take any steps to perform a search. Similar experiences are shared by my fellow career counsellors in India.

Career Selective Attention Focus

Through the opportunity awareness quiz and hands-on activities, we intend to bring to attention the various careers that children would otherwise not be able to keep on their choice radar.

I once wanted to buy a blue car. Suddenly, every day I walked down the streets of Dubai I saw only blue cars. What happened in a day? Did everyone purchase blue cars overnight? My selective attention allowed me to focus on the blue car which was not there earlier in my brain's attentive focus.

Sir Ebrall speaks ...

We attend to roughly 11 million bytes of information subconsciously per second out of which we only process about 50 bytes per second consciously. The information available about the various careers online is like noise. Allowing students to consciously sit a quiz allows various careers to come into their conscious scope. It is like opening a doorway of attention for the potential career choices for the future.

What is Our UCD?

Unlike a typical unique selling proposition (USP), our unique career discovery (UCD) is the application of the seven steps of the pyramid bundled in a program. We conduct week-long programs for students in high school allowing them to be handheld throughout the seven steps.

Our hybrid methodology of hands-on learning with career modules allows the children to understand the future path with distinct clarity.

We operate our process through programs in various schools and centres across the world. In our centres, we allow the kids to do fun hands-on activities following the quiz so that the learning is consolidated. Engaging the children is the best way to make them retain information. No amount of chalk and talk or reading would allow the consolidation of the information to happen as much as it does when engaging the children.

Neuroscience clearly explains a phenomenon called chunking.

We have developed an unbeatable experience over the years in executing the pyramid and in the process of helping thousands of students. We urge the stakeholders – i.e., teachers and parents – to embrace the pyramid as a proper methodological curriculum so that the children can benefit in the long run.

Sir Ebrall's tip:

Chunking is a strategy of breaking down the information into bite-sized pieces so that the brain can easily digest new information. The reason the brain needs this assistance is that the working memory can only attend to a limited amount of information for a limited time.

A classic example is the way that phone numbers are typically remembered or seen. A long string of numbers like 8002224950 overloads the cognitive working circuit. The best way to represent the phone number is 800-222-4950. This allows the registration and coding process in the working memory simultaneously.

800–1 Careers in an Hour: The Magical Formula

The results from *Mybraindesign*® allow seventeen different cognitive maps to be generated. Each map has a unique personality, behaviour traits, and career aspirations linked to it. We segregated 800 careers into well-formed career clusters matching the seventeen brain designs derived from the test.

We further integrated the eight thinking drivers that were originally adopted from the Neethling inventory to further identify micro-clusters of the careers. Dr. Kobus Neethling's work in whole-brain science has been commendable.

The divisions are quite metaphoric as the latest studies of positron emission tomography (PET) scans and functional magnetic resonance imaging (MRI) have disregarded the hemispheric divide. Although behavioural clues are clearly evident based on the dominant brain preferences. The idea is to tap the preferences so that one's personality and behavioural traits can be well understood.

Lifedesign Blueprint®

The *lifedesign blueprint*® is synthesised keeping the total process and progress of the career journey in mind. It is designed to explore all the relevant internal and external factors influencing career choices. It is designed as a simple display graph on which the details can be plotted and relevant decisions about the choices of extracurricular activity, subjects, curriculum choices, and further career path choices are mapped. The details are discussed in the forthcoming chapters.

1) Academic capabilities 2) Available course and subject options at school 3) Available extra-curricular options at school; extra hours at home	Map careers offered based on *Mybraindesign*® career cluster map here	1) Explore financial options 2) Family background; genetic influence; available resources to be explored 3) Opportunity to travel outside the city/country
	Identify interest-based career options and map here	
	Identify the common ones and highlight here	

FIGURE 11. DIAGRAM OF THE *LIFEDESIGN BLUEPRINT*® (DIAGRAM BY THE AUTHOR).

Hobby Crafting and Skill Gap Inventory: Do what is Relevant for Brain Growth

Successful people are able to develop a balance between non-cognitive and cognitive skills. The non-cognitive skills stem from the emotional parts of the brain. The skills of communication, empathy, support, and teamwork are all necessary.

The after-school hours are the best time in a child's life. There is an upbeat fashion globally of allowing children to do fifteen odd activities as extracurricular. This is essentially overwhelming their brain's learning circuits. The hobbies must be well chosen and crafted to suit the right type of cognitive growth. These should be offered in tandem with their cognitive preferences allowing the hobbies to fulfil the necessary cognitive preference gap. Hence, constantly bombarding the brain with doing various activities can be counterproductive for the growth of the child's brain.

We have defined various hobbies that can be linked to *Mybraindesign®*. The idea is to flow and grow. We want children to flow in their best cognitive brain preferences while growing in the opposing preferences.

Let me give a very simple example. If the child is highly rational in thinking and less emotional or empathetic, it is necessary that we provide enough rational stimulation through extracurricular activities like playing chess, maths Olympiad, playing bridge, etc. It is also important that they participate in social skill-building activities, such as team sports or social work. This will allow the balance of the flow and the grow of the brain.

Success Signatures: Mirror Neurons for Success

What is career success really? Is happiness equated to success? Is achievement equated to career success? Who is happy?

We amalgamated all such relevant questions into one major research question and took interviews with highly successful people in various fields. Some of the successful signatures are included in the addendum in the bonus chapter.

One very relevant thing to learn from our study is that successful people are the ones who align their thinking preferences to the work that they are doing. Some of them pivoted to the unrelated path in their careers as they understood the alignment well. We also figured out that most people used both sides of the brain's cognitive rational and limbic areas well enough. None of the success patterns indicated a skewed use.

By giving real-life examples to children, you are allowing their mirror neurons to fire. There are forward-feeding and rewind circuits in the brain, and it is necessary to kindle those for allowing the children to identify with the concept that one is teaching.

Children never learn from adults talking to them about success but by allowing them to interact and meet successful people. They learn more about the various career ups and downs through engaging in real life. They are always curious to meet new people and learn.

Teaching the Happiness Inquiry Routine

I also am a strong proponent of setting up a happiness inquiry routine at school or home. Teaching the difference between joy and pleasure is a must. Making them understand what provides them with happiness in the true sense is necessary. Providing adequate love, care, appreciation, and attention to the child's reward circuits of the brain is important.

Every Second is Crucial for the Young Brain

Allowing exploration at a young age is necessary. Exposing children to the vocabulary of various careers through hands-on processes and programs is important. Not choosing the right career path is not the end of the world, but succeeding here could definitely be the beginning of the world of change for a brighter future for the young Generation Alpha.

Let us explore the fundamental self-discovery methodology of *Mybraindesign*® in detail in the next chapter. It is a one-stop-shop tool for evaluating the aptitudes, preferences of thinking, personality, and behavioural traits of someone in pretty much a single assessment.

I bet you will be blown away by the results. One can predict the behaviours of the person quite appropriately. While it is not just limited to children, we, as adults can also be getting far-reaching insights into our thinking patterns.

Walk the talk

1. How do you define career success? Remember success can be subjective. It is necessary to think about it in your own headspace.

2. Why don't you try this experiment in your class if you're a teacher or at home if you're a parent? Ask your children to write as many careers as they know in a stipulated time interval. I bet you will understand the limited vocabulary of career choices that they indeed can speak about. Do it for yourself.

References

1. Business Standard. (2019, February 3). *Most students are aware of only 7 career options.* https://www.business-standard.com/article/pti-stories/most-students-aware-of-just-seven-career-options-study-119020300347_1.html

7
Mybraindesign®: The Secret Source to 'Know Thyself'

Knowing How You Think Decides How You Act and, Hence, How You Work and Live. It is Pure Mathematics

> 'Mastering others is strength.
> Mastering yourself is true power.'
>
> — LAO TZU

How do we determine what a child is capable of achieving in the future by merely taking a snapshot of their present thinking? We raised this important question earlier in the book. We also agreed on the fact that brain growth is dynamic. What makes us design something that is uncovering the potential through a simple assessment?

We believe in this profound statement: For building a successful life, self-discovery is the beginning and self-development is the continuum. The daunting task of selecting the best career for a high school or college graduate is made easy through the *Mybraindesign*® assessment.

Our major focus was on developing a neurodevelopmental tool that could offer us a headway in suggesting the right skills, extracurricular activities, and career choices. The proprietary assessment for determining the cognitive make is called *Mybraindesign*® because it is indicating the way the child thinks based on their brain's thinking style. The same tool is applicable to adults and post-college students (albeit with slightly different questions and styles of questions).

The brain design showcases the cognitive or thinking style that further determines the child's personality, work values, possible career choices, and most importantly their outlook on the work of tomorrow. No assessment is valid if it does not showcase what it is supposed to show (validity) or fails to show the same results when tested again (reliability). Our assessment has passed both rigorous tests. We have been offering this assessment globally for more than eight years now to thousands of students.

We take a slightly different approach to mapping out the cognitive flow patterns following the determination of the thinking types. Each person thinks uniquely, and it is important to map the person's strengths, opportunities, resistances, and techniques to overcome the resistances (SORT) through the *Mybraindesign*® analysis. The SORT allows us to sort through the career confusions.

Work is an important aspect of daily life. Having a career that provides the individual with an identity and resonates with their inner calling is the right career. A career is perceived as a series of individual attitudes and behaviours and integrated work-related activities during the life of a person.

I have understood that money, success, or fame can offer transient joy, but inner contentment and fulfilment are all that matter at the end of the day. I do not mean to say that one should not have a career that does not provide sufficient material prosperity.

Striking the Right Balance is Key

I am living testimony of the *Mybraindesign*® assessment. Undertaking the assessment made me realise my SORT, which allowed me to navigate my career to its desired destination. I would have still been testing and trying various career paths if I had not embraced the assessment at the right time.

The time loss in the process of hunting for the right path can be huge. This time loss can translate into a material loss. We often see students opting to spend years finding out their best fit. This time lost is very crucial. They lose the opportunity for being trained and exposed to the world of work. Would you as a stakeholder want your child to experiment and go through the time-opportunity juggle? Or do you want to be well informed and receive the help of validated scientific tools helping the child navigate the various paths with ease?

We Live This Belief

We believe everyone can do anything but to do the one exact thing that he or she is carved out for makes a world of difference in embracing success. Our program highlights the requirements of success signatures aligned to various career paths. It is one of the celebrated programs in schools in Asia and the Middle East.

The Human Brain is Nothing Short of the Eighth Wonder of the World

The human brain is a wonder (Figure 12). It weighs only 1.4kg but contains over one hundred billion neurons. It would take over thirty-five years (twenty-four/seven) to count each and every single cell in the brain individually. The brain's memory storage is in petabytes. You would have to put your television on for over 300 years to exhaust the brain's complete and total memories. Each brain cell or neuron connects to about 10,000 adjoining neurons called synapses. The total number of combinations would be one followed by over 10.5 million zeroes.

The potential of the brain is huge. New technologies like PET scan, single-photon emission computed tomography (SPECT), MRI, and electroencephalogram (EEG) have helped us to learn the finer details about the brain. The experiments on the brain have become ultra-sophisticated. The diversity of thinking is huge.

- ❖ Human brains weigh about 1.3 to 1.4 kilograms
- ❖ The cerebrum is 85% of the total brain weight
- ❖ The human brain is made up of 60% fat
- ❖ It uses about 20% of oxygen in our blood
- ❖ It uses up about 25% of glucose supply
- ❖ The brain's consistency is comparable to tofu
- ❖ The brain is composed of about 100 billion neurons
- ❖ 5 to 10 minutes of oxygen loss can to lead to damage

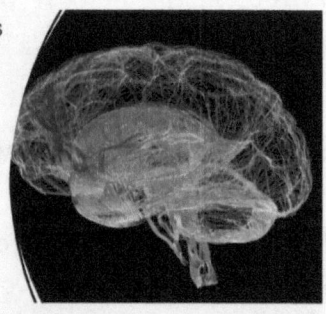

FIGURE 12. FACTS ABOUT THE BRAIN (VARIOUS SOURCES COMBINED).

Even Twins Think Differently

Everyone has a unique way of thinking. Twins, with seemingly similar biology, have distinct thought patterns.

Our thinking styles influence our career choices.

If you are a step-by-step thinker, computer programming or coding is ideally suited for you.

If you prefer working with people, working as a graphic designer may not be suitable. The diversity of thinking is well captured by the *Mybraindesign*® map. The assessment allows everyone to become self-aware of their cognitive functioning and patterns of thinking.

Being Self-Aware is Rare

Did you know that 95% of people think and claim that they are self-aware while indeed only ten to fifteen per cent are self-aware? It is quite common not to understand the science of the self fully. People may have perceived notions about the self but verbalising it without the help of a structured tool is an issue.

Nature or Nurture?

I am often asked a question in my seminars, does nature or nurture impact brain design? My answer is very clear and scientific. Both have an impact. One can argue over the percentages for each, but the clear thing is indeed *nature + nurture* = **brain design**.

There are subtle variations in the thinking patterns of each individual. Genetic factors along with the environment contribute to the development of the final design map.

No Pop Neuroscience

Simplifying the science to a level where it flies with its subtle misinterpreted nuances is pop science. Oversimplification of the concept can, in essence, kill the concept. I am a huge proponent of whole-brain science because I have lived with it. I have experimented with it. It is no more a theory in my life.

The whole-brain science is a concept that essentially means you are not watertight in your thinking patterns of being right-side brained or left. You essentially have both sides of the brain, be it left or right. It is only merely the way you are wired that the patterns of thinking vary.

You Can Dissect the Brain But can you Dissect the thoughts?

The brain is complex and one needs to understand its simplified functioning in a proper way or method. It is necessary to take the functioning as a metaphor. You can dissect the brain, but you cannot dissect the thought. There is already enough debate about the accurate and perfect positioning of the mind within the brain or body. We have not yet unfolded some of the mysteries of the universe.

The background for the assessment relies on the fundamental cognitive science that the brain is formed of two parts – cognitive and limbic (Figure 13). The rational brain allows us to focus on the task and think logically and find the solutions to the problems. The limbic system or the emotional brain is impulsive. It is where our basic instinctive and motivational behaviours arise. Further, there are four fundamental lobes of the brain. The frontal part, also called the frontal lobe, is responsible for judgment, planning, memory, speech, and execution. The portions at the back of the brain, the occipital area, are responsible for visuospatial processing. The parietal lobe is vital for sensory perception and integration, including the management of taste, hearing, sight, touch, and smell. It is home to the brain's primary somatic sensory cortex, a region where the brain interprets input from other areas of the body. The temporal lobe is responsible for the comprehension of sounds.

To simplify and explain the concept further, let's say if someone tries to annoy you, and you feel like shouting at them this is your limbic system firing, while if you keep your composure this is your prefrontal cortex intervention. If you want to make a decision or choice, upon the effective visualisation of the options from the back portion of the brain, your front part evaluates the pros and cons to help you decide.

Sir Ebrall speaks ...

It is a myth that we use about ten per cent of the brain. The neurons or brain cells are always firing all the time.

Scientists looked very hard to find what was so special in Einstein's brain. Nothing major was found except that his brain was slightly wider in the area allowing for spatial reasoning. This is not uncommon to see such differences for us as well.

Funny laugh: Albert Einstein, the Nobel prize-winning physicist who gave the world the theory of relativity, $E = mc^2$, and the law of the photoelectric effect, obviously had a special brain. So special that when he died in Princeton Hospital, on April 18, 1955, the pathologist on call, Thomas Harvey, stole it.

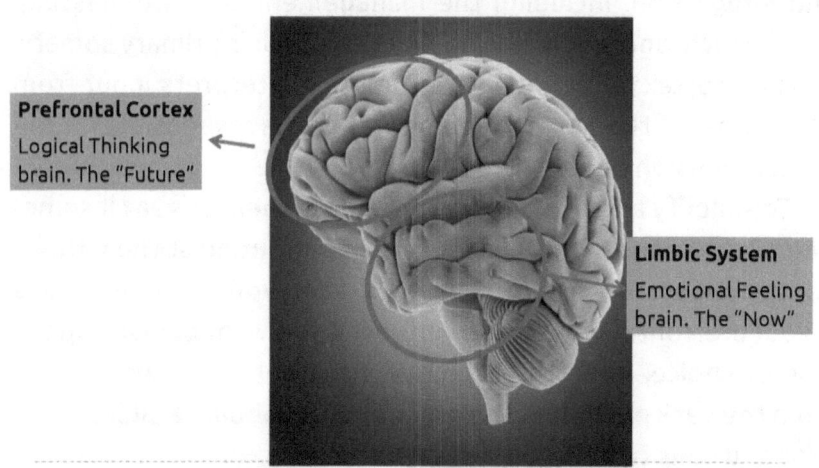

FIGURE 13. DRAWING OF THE RATIONAL AND LIMBIC BRAIN (IMAGE BY THE AUTHOR).

All That Glitters Through Cognitive Science is Only Gold

In personal life and also for organisations, the quantity and quality of our cognitive behaviours – i.e., those associated with activities of thinking, learning, problem-solving, and decision-making – produce a dramatic effect on performance, productivity and potential for growth.

Many of the cognitive style theories that have been developed are linked to the left-/right-side of the brain thinking, which follows the bipolarity pattern that indicates a person sits on a spectrum at one of the ends or somewhere in the continuum.

While the left side of the brain is considered linear, analytical, sequential, rational and goal-oriented, the right side is seen as more intuitive, spontaneous, holistic, emotional, and visual.

Applications of these theories in a practical output allow us to simplify the understanding. There have been millions of profiles performed with the Herrmann Brain Dominance Instrument (HBDI). The majority of the Fortune 500 companies are well aware of the Herrmann inventory or have used it for their staff and recruiters. The Neethling inventory is available in more than twenty-five different outputs. We can map one's brain to the desired outcome of parenting style, spirituality style, business relationship style, etc.

Personality – A mathematical Formula as an Output of Thinking

Our personality means the way we operate in the world. It is nothing but our unique way of thinking about things and behaving and reacting to situations. Our personalities are often consistent throughout our lives once established, unless one really works hard to mould them differently. Personalities can never be described as good or bad, right or wrong, only different.

Personality types at least partially determine the fit for some career types.

If you hate making quick decisions, you might be dreadful at being a paramedic who has to make decisions in split seconds. The university or school can build those skills, but skills last longer when your personality and thinking are aligned.

The Big Four: *Mybraindesign*® Assessment

Our assessment's purpose is to bring forth a clear understanding of the dominant functioning of the individual child's brain. The two parts of the brain as clearly defined above have a unique process and method of reasoning. The limbic brain is all about reasoning, while the cognitive or rational brain is all about processing.

Anatomical Correlation to the Types of the Thinking

Indeed the anatomical correlation with each part of the brain and the type of the thinking is quite obvious. The front portions of the brain are responsible for the type 1 thinking while the parietal and occipital brains link with type 2 thinking. The limbic cortex takes care of the type 3 and 4 thinking.

Figure 14 summarises the processes and reasoning related to each of its halves. Each type of thinking is labelled 1 to 4 in a chronological fashion.

The *Mybraindesign*® maps are visual representations of a person's cognitive or thinking preferences as expressed through the answers provided in the questionnaire.

They aim to study the behavioural patterns emerging out of the thinking types. The person's expressed preferences in each of the thinking types are mapped. The chronological flow maps are designed once the dominant thinking types are mapped. Further, the eight dimensions of thinking are plotted. This allows the child to understand the best-fit careers by plotting a career cluster graph.

Mybraindesign®, therefore, does not apply a fixed label to the thinking types but allows a dynamic cognitive thinking flow map to develop. Essentially, it provides a powerful visual explanation for why children or adults approach situations in a particular way.

The remarkable complexity of the brain has shown that human beings cannot credibly be divided up into a fixed number of types or groups of people who are unable to act outside of their cognitive abilities.

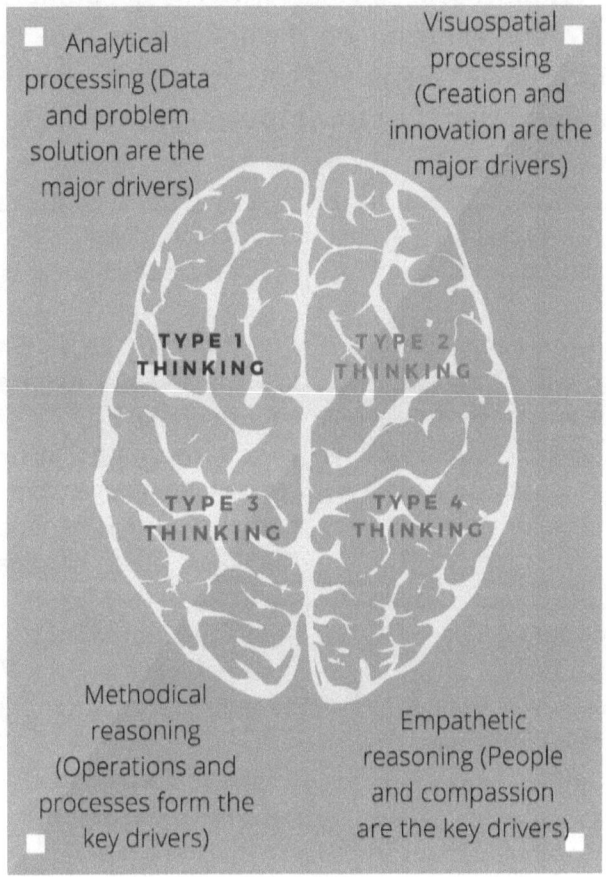

FIGURE 14. IMAGE OF THE FOUR TYPES IN THE *MYBRAINDESIGN®* MAP.

There are no watertight boundaries in each of the processing quadrants. One can have a mix of all processing types at once while another may just be dominant in the analytical processing. Further deriving a chronological map from the four types provides a cognitive processing flow map. The chronological path decides the way we think and solve problems. It determines our values.

Seventeen different cognitive processing maps are generated. **Each is represented below with the quadrant diagrams a unique representation of the individual thought flows (Figure 15).** The behaviour and actions arising from the thinking upon presenting the same problem are unique to each of the flow maps.

Type 1 Analytical processing	Type 2 Visuospatial processing
Type 1 thinkers adopt a data-driven approach. They are often cautious, correct, detail-oriented, thorough, unassuming, logical, systematic, and quality-oriented. Silence is golden for them. Their favourite sayings: 'If the trail does not match the map. There is something wrong with the trail.' 'Where did you read that and what edition was that?'	Type 2 thinkers have their heads in the clouds and bringing them back to reality is a task. They are creative, outgoing, flexible, creative, communicative, and optimistic. They see opportunities where others see dead ends. Their favourite sayings: 'I am up to try and experiment.' 'I have all the resources and happy to collaborate.'

Type 3 Methodical reasoning	Type 4 Empathetic reasoning
The very prominent thinking style is methodical reasoning. They are detail-oriented, methodical, highly organised, time-bound, loyal and process-driven. Detailed review is normal. Their favourite sayings: 'Do not give me a vague output.' 'The devil is in the details.'	The very prominent thinking style hovers around processing emotions and helping. They are friendly, kind, helpful, always willing to work in teams, empathetic and people-driven. Working together in a team is bliss. Their favourite sayings: 'Let us make this world a better place.' 'Let us extend our help to those who need it.'

FIGURE 15. QUADRANT DIAGRAM OF THE FOUR TYPES IN THE *MYBRAINDESIGN*® MAP.

Spot the Celebrity

FIGURE 16. OPRAH WINFREY (IMAGE COURTESY OF GOOGLE IMAGES, COPYRIGHT FREE).

Can you think of examples of celebrities who are dominant thinkers in each of these types? I can think of Bill Gates as a type 1 + 2 thinker. Well, Oprah Winfrey (Figure 16) and Coco Chanel are dominant type 2 thinkers. While Mother Teresa and Mahatma Gandhi were dominant type 4 thinkers. Can you come up with examples for type 3 thinkers?

Spot Your Colleagues or Family Members

A few months back I met a businessman in relation to our proprietary Contributory Success Signature program. He was a complete type 1 thinker. He spared thirty-five minutes for me. He was on time. He had his constant gaze on the watch as we started to speak. He neither offered coffee nor tea.

He examined my business card pretty thoroughly. He was already sceptical of the program, which I could gauge from his body language. He was quite dry in his conversation. While I explained the finest details (remember I am a type 2 + 3 thinker) with complete enthusiasm. My body language was all over the place while the gentleman sat still in his chair.

The next day I sent him a detailed mail as requested at his end for the same. As expected, I got a very meticulous reply in bullet points about his opinion on the program. Just precise and to the point mail as you would expect from a type 1 thinker.

Remember That Type 1 Thinkers Always Have Their Point of View

Let me share some of my interactions with type 2 + 3 thinkers. Strangely, in my life, I keep coming across them a lot. I had a colleague of mine at work who was totally a Mr. Resource. You could call him for anything even middle of the night and he would surely attend and provide you with the requisite information. He was always up. Never tired of having a conversation. He was always thinking big. He never cared about the data.

Not that he did not pay attention to the data. People and innovative ideas have more value over the data. The meetings with the board members were dreadful for him. The type 1 thinkers in the boardroom would pounce on him for silly things. I think those minute non-specific details were out of his brain's radar.

Well, remember that they are always ready to come up with an innovative solution. Will they work on it? I strongly doubt it because science says it is hard for them to implement and act.

Think of examples of type 3 and 4 thinkers in your own life. Can you draw a mental persona of these dominant thinkers? How they behave, talk, make decisions, have relationships, the way their workplaces are, the way they write emails, send notes, etc. Each of their minutest behaviour links back to their dominant thinking type.

I would urge you to use this understanding to spot the thinking profiles of your colleagues, friends, relatives, and boss or supervisor at work. It is a fun exercise. I have become so good at it over the years.

Even in my medical practice, I could spot the left-/right-side or rational/limbic brains without any issues. This makes my life easy because now my behaviour mirrors theirs and they feel extremely comfortable. Of course, I may not be able to guess a complete cognitive flow pattern for which I do need a detailed brain analysis before a fair idea about the dominant thinking types to emerge for a subject. This leads me to cater my offerings to suit their personality type.

Remember, the brain always likes to see similarities and be comfortable. The brain is super smart in conserving energy. It does not like to expend a dime extra on daily living. Just take a moment and think about the people in your lives who match your thinking types.

We have done a ton of real-life interviews and tried to relate the various professions and job roles to the types of thinking profiles (Figures 18 and 19). We have also created a profession map based on our analysis.

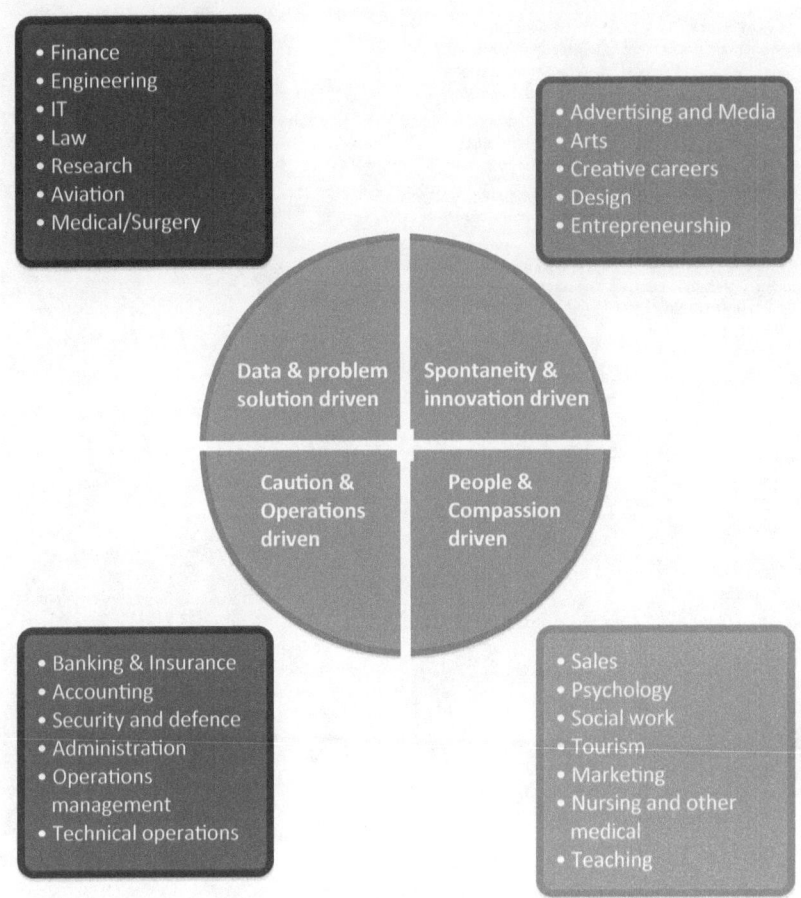

FIGURE 17. PROFESSIONS MAP BASIC BASED ON THE BIG FOUR THINKING TYPES (DIAGRAM BY THE AUTHOR).

Finance: Financial Manager, Banker, Stock Exchange Trader	Engineering: Aeronautics, Electronics, Telecommunications, Oil, Data Processing	Design: Architect, Designer, Decorator Webmaster, Web Designer	
Geography: Geography, Surveyor CAD Drafter	Aviation: Technician, Pilot Air Traffic Controller	Sales: Salesperson, Sales Manager Real Estate, Medical Rep	Creation: Script Writer, Fashion Designer
IT: Networking, Technician System Analyst	Research: Biologist, Chemist, Botanist	Advertising	Arts: Painter, Sculptor Musician
Medicine: Veterinary, Surgeons Doctor, Ophthalmologist, Physiotherapist, Radiologist, Dentist	**Analyzes** **Is logical** **Is critical** **Is realistic**	**Infers** **Takes risks** **Is impetuous** **Breaks rules**	Marketing: Research, Product Manager
Law: Lawyer, Judge, Notary, Bailiff	**Knows about money** **Knows how things work** **Quantifies/Likes numbers**	**Likes surprises** **Is curious/Plays** **Speculates/Imagines**	Film Making: Actor, Editor
Insurance: Insurance Broker	**Takes preventive action** **Establishes procedures** **Gets things done**	**Is sensitive to others** **Likes to teach** **Touches a lot**	Journalism: Journalist, Copy Reader, Designer
Administration: Assistant, Personal Assistant, Office Clerk	**Plans/Organizes** **Is reliable** **Is neat** **Timely**	**Is supportive** **Is expressive** **Talks a lot** **Feels**	Teaching: Teacher, University Professor
Accounting: CPA, Book-Keeper, Organizational Manager, Economist	Security: Fireman, Policeman Security Guard	Tourism: Flight Attendant, Tourist Guide, Receptionist, Translator/Interpreter, Tourist Information Facility Manager	Medical: Paediatric Nurse, Dietician, Nurse, Midwife, Speech Therapist, Occupational Therapist
Governmental: Tax Auditor Administrator OSHA Inspector			Human Resources: Trainer, HR Manager
		Marketing: Public Relations	Psychology: Psychologist Career Counsellor
			Social Workers: Clinical Social Worker, Educator, Family Advisor, Case Manager

FIGURE 18. PROFESSIONS MAP (ADVANCED) RELATED TO THE THINKING TYPES (IMAGE BY THE AUTHOR).

Deep Diving into the Work Values

> A very well-known quote on work values is this:
> 'I don't know what I want, but I know it's not this.'
>
> — JULIE JANSEN

Values are the standards by which we evaluate the importance of things or activities. Values are a matter of what guides you through every day, every task, and every encounter with another human being. One's purpose in life has a lot to do with what kind of impact one wants to make in the world. Examples of work values are achievement, independence, recognition, relationships, helping, contributing to a cause, etc.

Values serve as a compass to keep us focused on what is most important and assist us in making the right decisions. Hence, it is important that values as well as personality factor into the decision-making process and the preparations we and our children make for the world of work.

The values in each of the thinking types are enumerated below. Tick the boxes you think apply to you which could indicate your thinking types also.

The Power of AI for the 21st Century

We have further utilised the power of artificial intelligence to compute various indices (Figure 19) obtained through the results of the cognitive index and flow maps. The work value index and the environment suitability indices are helpful in further refining career choices.

An indicator reflecting 'high' to 'low' is presented to the child under each category. The stakeholder can learn about it and get an understanding of the child's preferences.

The work value index focuses on the subtle values each area of work entails while the environmental suitability index helps to focus on the country and university choice. Here are some of the outputs exemplifying the indices.

Leadership Index
The ability to lead is an important factor. This can mean embracing leadership qualities like taking charge, developing novel path-breaking ideas, leading a team or leading oneself.

Team Collaboration Index
Teamwork is the collaborative effort of a group to achieve a common goal or to complete a task in the most effective and efficient way. Team collaboration capability is defined as one of the most important abilities for an individual. Higher score means higher ability.

21st Century Agility Index
Agility is more than just being able to react well to change. In today's world, an individual need to continuously keep discovering ways of working which are better suited to situations and continue adapting for the better. Higher score entails higher agility.

Career Stability Index
Being able to stick to a career path which is chosen for a long time. Most people in the world would find it hard to remain faithful to a career for a long time. People with high index score are comfortable in embracing one career for a longer period.

Gig Work Potential Index
A gig economy is a free market in which individuals earn income from on-demand, short term assignments, or jobs. Gigs are not full-time employees. The person with higher index is likely to seek Gig work in future. Gig economy workers are not employees but self-employee independent contract workers-often working for variety of clients.

FIGURE 19. VARIOUS INDICES DERIVED AS OUTPUT FROM THE THINKING PROCESSES OF THE BRAIN (IMAGE BY THE AUTHOR).

The Process Drivers

Each of the thinking dominances is further divided into two distinct process drivers. There can be unlimited combinations based on the dominant process drivers. The fact that each person is unique means that each person carries a unique thinking signature. The process drivers are established with a separate twelve-question mediated survey. This survey has a fixed choice problem provided to the brain so that the best driver linked to a particular behaviour shall be evident.

Each of the process drivers for each type of thinking is presented in the illustration (Figure 20). One of the drivers indicates action-oriented behaviour while the other one indicates internal motivation.

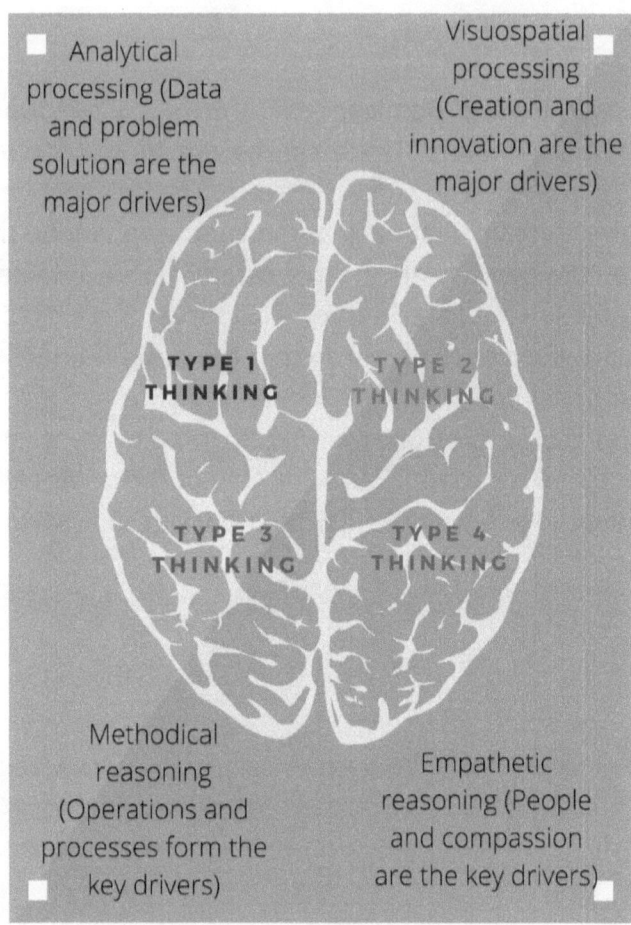

FIGURE 20. IMAGE OF THE DRIVERS ASSOCIATED WITH THE FOUR THINKING TYPES.

Does Cognitive Preference Equal Competence?

What we have seen through this chapter concerns the thinking styles. They are also labelled as cognitive preferences. One has to not confuse it with competence. Let me give you an example of my brain design. I am a strong type 2 + 3 thinker while my day job entails seeing patients which is a pure type 4 activity combined with type 1 thinking. While I am pretty good at what I do because of the skills and competencies that I have developed over time. However, I am more comfortable doing something creative or organising something through my dominant thinking types.

Let me share a simple analogy that I share with my students. Assume you have a very fancy blazer that you bought for a party. You would want to restrict its use only for the party. You would not want to wear that at home all time, even though it's your favourite. You wear it as necessary and once back home you comfortably wear your pyjamas. In a similar way, you develop skills in the brain's non-dominant portions. The moment you finish your work, and you are in your own headspace, you leave those developed skills and competencies in the locked room of your brain. You now start thinking and living your true preferences.

Someone may judge looking at you that you are a very meticulous and neat type 3 personality while you may actually be showcasing this due to the need of the hour – i.e., a party. Indeed, you may be a type 2 personality back home with your closet being completely shabby. It is possible to gauge the thinking styles from the personality, but you have to be very vigilant and use as many datasets of observation as possible. The way the person writes, speaks, answers, sits, makes gestures, etc., are all critical.

A very clear body language map may be derived from each of the thinking types. Let me showcase some of the body gestures for each of the styles in Figure 21.

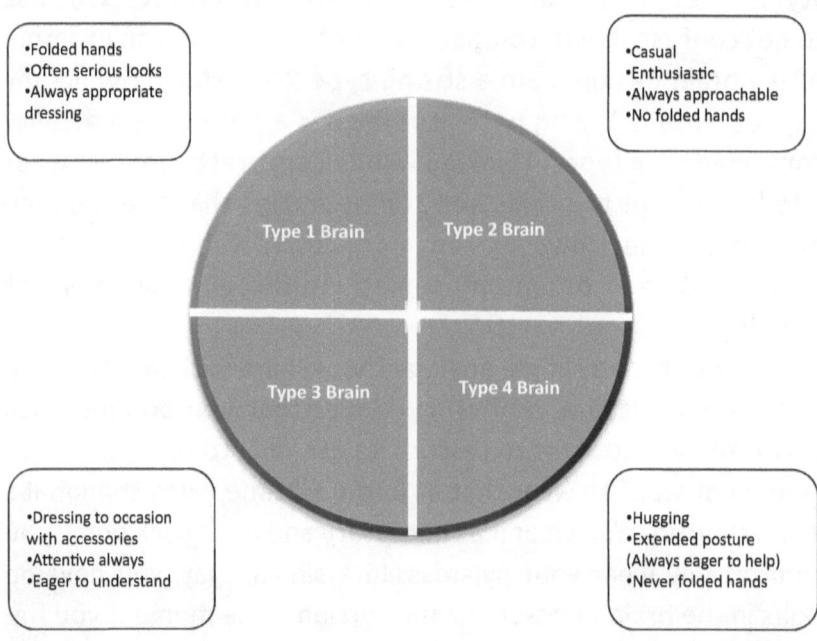

FIGURE 21. DIAGRAM OF BODY LANGUAGE MAP (IMAGE BY THE AUTHOR).

Our preferences represent those thinking styles that provide the greatest satisfaction and engage us most in our professional and personal lives. One may be competent in a particular process, however, not prefer that process in daily living. The clear outcome of this would be career fatigue or burnout over a long period of time.

The Right Age for *Mybraindesign*®

The *Mybraindesign*® output consolidates by the age of thirteen. Hence, the best age for assessment is when the child is in eighth grade or around thirteen years old. The assessment takes about half an hour to complete. The assessment absolutely has no right or wrong answers. It is available through an online link. The appendix at the end of the chapter provides the requisite links. There is no upper age limit and an adult version of the test is also available.

The Testimony of Science

Mybraindesign® is a twenty-five-question survey. Each answer is rated based on the choice made. The points are devised keeping in mind the overall score balance between the four output components. This tool is self-analysis and, hence, most people immediately recognise their results as accurate. It is a descriptive and non-judgemental analysis with no assessment being better or worse. The individual report provides a description of the child's thinking preferences and makes further recommendations based on the analysis from the AI-based model.

The test is reliable once it can be reproduced each time. The test also needs to measure what it is supposed to measure, which is statistically known as validity. The validity is further reinforced by having special correlations tests undertaken with the MBTI, DiSC, and NBI.

The idea was to extrapolate the findings to match the standard psychometric analysis. For the prospective studies involving more than 100 students, each of the students was offered the best career choice from the career cluster and a structured interview was carried out indicating their insights about the choice.

Both retrospective and prospective studies were carried out layering the cognitive maps to the desired career choices. Each of the clusters was then cross-correlated to the findings from Neethling's inventory. Twenty samples from real-world and successful top executives were compared to their cognitive preferences helping us to define the validity of the tool even further. Occupational mix correlation was performed on a sample of twenty-five different profiles of work. A blind interview was carried out giving an insight into the subject's satisfaction which was further matched to the results of the assessment.

Careerpik: Making a Career Choice Becomes a Sci-fi Experiment

The main aim of this book is to facilitate and help readers to select the right career choice for children and students. We have spent the majority of the time so far talking about self-discovery. Yes, we believe 80% of the decision is only about self-inquiry, the remaining 20% of effort further refines the career choices. The special module called *careerpik* is developed to help the stakeholders filter the final choices from a predetermined 800 separate careers and programs. This module facilitates the choice of career for the student. The complete *careerpik* module is available in our online surveys and assessment.

The *careerpik* module has four major career clusters and eight minor clusters. The child can filter his or her own interests to get the best fit career by navigating through the module.

Each of the major clusters is presented in Figure 22.

Type 1	Type 2
Analytical processing	Visuospatial and auditory processing
Data and solutions-oriented careers.	Entrepreneurship and creative careers. Business, leadership, theatre
Data sciences, computers, accounts	
Type 3	**Type 4**
Method-based reasoning	Empathetic reasoning
Operations and organisation-based careers. Management in business, law, military	Compassionate and people-facing careers. Teaching, nursing, media & marketing

FIGURE 22. QUADRANT DIAGRAM OF THE FOUR TYPES IN THE *MYBRAINDESIGN*® MAP AND ASSOCIATED MAJOR CAREER CLUSTERS.

Let me give you an example. If your child is a type 4 dominant empathetic reasoning thinker, it is easy to offer any of the above career choices. While if the child is interested in medicine, you validate the same and encourage the child to work towards the field of medicine. This is a very crude example but once you get a hang of the formula, it becomes easy to decide the careers.

Real-life Applications Beyond Careers

The assessment acts as a magician even helping beyond the choice of the right career. Planning a hobby, studying style, sports, etc., becomes child's play when the map is clearly read and understood. The most natural form of problem-solving strategy, communication style, behaviour, studying and learning style, relationship, and sporting style as uncovered in each of the types of thinking is outlined in Table 1.

TABLE 1. VARIOUS STYLES IN DETAILS

Styles	Analytical processing	Visuospatial processing	Methodical reasoning	Empathetic reasoning
Thinking style	These people are factual and analytical. They love dissecting the data. They enjoy crunching numbers. They are often precise in the information they provide. They seldom make any errors in measurements. They understand concepts related to technology fairly quickly.	These people are big picture people. They are excellent at predicting new possibilities. They are out of the box types. They like ideas. They thrive on inventing unusual solutions to problems. They have a so-called 'gut feel' for problems.	These people are well organised. They approach the problems practically and are always fine-print readers. They are meticulous and stand firm on the issues. They love supervision and roles that like monitoring.	These are focused people that love to be with others. They can sense how others feel. They understand the emotional meaning of body language. They have the ability to motivate others. Their understanding of human nature is their strength.

Styles	Analytical processing	Visuospatial processing	Methodical reasoning	Empathetic reasoning
Learning and studying style	They are usually solo learners. They ask pointed questions. They want only relevant information. They do not like elaborate answers. They love problem-solving. They are fascinated often by numbers and calculations. They like to read once thoroughly. They do not repeat unless necessary.	The people with this preference hate to sit still. They can be kinetic. They are usually quick learners. They are curious and love new things. They love multimedia and story-based learning. They often learn in groups. They can be impulsive. They may be too fast in studying and learning, often overlooking some parts.	These people love methodical approaches to learning. They take elaborate notes. They ask many questions to make sure that they know exactly what to do and how to do it. They thrive on orderly step-by-step instructions.	People and group learning is their passion. They love to help or take help from others while learning. They are responsive and sensitive. Their learning is often dependent on the teacher. Their relation to teachers means the world to them.

Styles	Analytical processing	Visuospatial processing	Methodical reasoning	Empathetic reasoning
Communication style	These people are to the point speakers. They do not like to beat about the bush. They love to be backed by facts as they speak. They do not like vague talk. They are focused as they speak and look into the eye of others as they speak.	They love unconventional communication. They love using metaphors. They tend to think faster than they speak. They can jump from one topic to another. They are quite dramatic in their presentations.	Communication among these people is quite orderly, factual and well-focused. They are quite inflexible and have to finish what they start saying. They want to know each and every detail.	These people love talking and normally use sympathetic and supporting words. They are thoughtful listeners. They try to never hurt anyone. They choose their words wisely. They are good verbal communicators.
Problem-solving style	They make sense of any problem before they argue. They gather facts and logic. They are barely driven by emotions. Their way is often considered the best way. They can be vindictive. They like to analyse and solve a problem rather than bring out an intuition-based solution.	They approach problems in an intuitive way. They struggle with people who sulk and love to take risks. They prefer to have their say and get arguments over pretty quickly.	They deal with the problem in a chronological way. They like to gather all the facts and examine them thoroughly. They do not form judgements. They use tried and tested methods to solve the problem.	The main aspect for these people is feelings. They feel overly emotional for a problem that they may miss the rational solutions. They can overreact in a crisis. They hate confrontation and any kind of emotional discomfort.

Styles	Analytical processing	Visuospatial processing	Methodical reasoning	Empathetic reasoning
Sports style	Individual sports are preferred. They study the opponent's moves in detail. They keep practising until they make it perfect. They apply what is thought best and hate making a mistake.	They play out of the ordinary sports. They like sports but participate in their own way. They like to form their own rules. They are flexible enough that they can change the rules to fit the outcome.	They are devoted team players. They love playing team sports. They will practice until they are perfect in every step. They have fixed game plans. They stick to their routine quite rigidly.	These people love to participate in team sports. The team members are important to them. They show a lot of passion, and their enthusiasm keeps their energy levels high. They are good at managing team conflicts and easing emotions in the team.

What About the Underutilised Thinking Preferences?

The majority of the people in our study had two strong preferences of thinking followed by three. Very few people had a combination of all the four thinking types acting in combination (we call this a box design).

The best analogy is to look forward through the windscreen as you are driving a car. This is your dominant thinking style and flow map, but you also use your rear mirror to double-check that you are on the right track. The less preferred thinking preferences are like your rear mirrors. They play an important part to warn you so that you do not venture out into the wrong territory.

We have met so many kids who chose careers in the under-utilised thinking patterns and had a miserable graduation life or college life.

To sustain a positive passion and be happy, one has to be aligned with their cognitive preferences and the demands of the job or career they have selected. The *Mybraindesign*® tool, in essence, is the synopsis or summary of a person's thinking preferences at a specific time in his or her life.

A banker who is not analytical or method oriented cannot survive the chores of banking for long. While a doctor who is oriented only to visuospatial processing may not find medicine fulfilling.

The Most Relevant Asked Question

Before we move on, let me raise an essential question. This is the most asked question in my sessions globally. Can you change your brain's thinking style? I want you to spend some time thinking over this.

Yes, you can change your thinking types. However, it is a task. You need to consciously work for years to achieve this. It is not easy to move quickly from being an x type of thinker to a y type. It is hard work. Once the thinking pattern is consolidated at the age of thirteen, it does take serious work. Any major challenges in life, exposure to a crisis, death, etc., can quickly change the pattern but otherwise, it is a process.

The whole idea of this exercise is not to draw a picture-perfect box design with all four types of thinking but to understand the strengths and resistances arising out of the same. The idea of developing a tool that affords us an insight into our thinking processes is that we can start to work on the non-preferred side from the start and further allow our best part to align with our life and career choices. The bonus chapter describes this *flow and grow* concept with further clarity.

More About the Box Design and Cognitive process flow maps

Box design essentially means that there is equally distributed processing and reasoning in the four parts of the brain. Is this helpful or hurtful? The next chapter allows you to ponder over the question more as it showcases the various **cognitive process flow maps** and describes the strengths and resistances (SORT) of each of the designs in great detail.

A detailed SORT chart and a career cluster overlay are available for each of the maps. So, hang tight and see the magic unfold. The career clusters and the maps will give a very clear view of the utility of *Mybraindesign*® in the career unfolding process.

Walk the talk

1. How many thinking types do we house in our brains? Describe the personality and behaviour of each of the types of thinking brains.
2. Picture your spouse, children, or boss – which type of thinking brain is dominant among them?
3. Celebrity map – draw the thinking map for your favourite celebrity to consolidate the learning of the thinking types.

8

The End Point for Your Career Choice is the New Beginning for Your Life

Aligning the Career Clusters to the *Mybraindesign*® Maps and the Thinking Flow Maps with the SORT Chart Will Be Like Aligning the Most Important Part of Life's Puzzles in the Right Order

'Make sure in ten years you say that you chose your life, and you did not settle for it.'

— ROB HILL

We have approximately eight billion people on this planet and our minds are capable of thinking more than 50,000 thoughts a day. Just imagine the permutations and combinations of thinking patterns that can be developed based on the eight drivers and seventeen different preference maps.

No two individuals think the same way. Their motivations and interests are different and so too the way they think and act. This chapter ties up the information obtained from the *Mybraindesign*® map to the final career choices. A person can have any of the unique seventeen types of the thinking map. The person's behaviour, personality, choices, etc., can be confidently predicted once the thinking map is available.

A highly sophisticated AI-based algorithm determines the final choices in our online assessment. This chapter highlights the simple methodology behind the complex formula. The major and minor career clusters help in narrowing the career choices from the vast selection of 800 careers that we have adopted in our career pyramid.

No Easy Task

Narrowing from thousands of careers to the chosen few in a cluster was a mammoth task for me. I have closely considered each of the career paths and their functions aligning to the job specifics. I have also validated these choices by doing real-life interviews with people employed in the professions.

I also undertook a detailed prospective evaluation of the choices as picked by our students and followed them until the end of their graduation to know how satisfied and content they were in picking these choices.

I entrusted the task also to fellow research colleagues at my institute. As we started this task, we were surprised to find thousands of course options in each career. We hunted for the best go-to sources on the internet. We did not leave any resources untapped. We interviewed university professors, career coaches, and counsellors. It took us five years to work on the final 800 career types of the cluster map.

We had to learn about each of the courses and interview the students studying them to understand and know about the courses. The researchers would speak for hours with each of the candidates from Australia to Canada making sure that the course overview is well researched.

It was a big job. But for us, the idea behind it was very simple. We wanted every child's journey to be smooth. We wanted to be near exhaustive in our selection of the clusters.

This chapter highlights the various thinking flow maps emerging from the fundamental drivers of thinking. The unique SORT chart pertaining to each of the types of thinking is presented. A master career cluster design will help in narrowing down individual choices. Let's get into it!

Recap From the Last Chapter

Cognitive models are powerful thinking tools or metaphors. When these models are understood they can enhance communication, teamwork, and decision-making, which can again enhance effective problem-solving.

Flexible, critical, and creative problem-solving skills are necessary in a rapidly changing world in order to cope with and find solutions for its many problems. Deciding on whether to start or not to start a venture is an example of such a problem-solving situation faced by the entrepreneur. A habitual entrepreneur has a unique mindset that allows them to identify not only more opportunities but also unique ones. They are driven by type 2 thinking.

This is the simple idea behind the *Mybraindesign*® thinking maps.

The *Mybraindesign*® assessment's purpose is to bring forth a clear understanding of how a person thinks. It brings forth the way they analyse problems. It also narrates how each of the parts of the brain engages in a way to bring forward a solution for any problem and identifies how a person communicates, engages in relationships, behaves in a particular set up of circumstances, and more.

The Big Four Assessment (Figure 23)

Type 1 Analytical processing (Data is the major driver)	Type 2 Visuospatial processing (Creativity is the major driver)
Type 3 Methodical reasoning (Process is the major driver)	Type 4 Empathetic reasoning (People are the key drivers)

FIGURE 23. QUADRANT DIAGRAM OF THE BIG FOUR ASSESSMENT.

The Drivers of Thinking (Figure 24)

Type 1 Analytical processing (Frontal) Data-driven Solution-focussed	Type 2 Visuospatial and auditory processing (Parieto-Occipital) Creative Enterprising
Type 3 Method-based reasoning (Frontal & Limbic) Cautious Operations-driven	Type 4 Empathetic reasoning (Limbic) People-driven Compassionate

FIGURE 24. QUADRANT DIAGRAM OF THE FOUR DRIVERS OF THINKING.

SORT Charts: A Unique Snapshot Overviewing the Strengths and Weakness

The SORT chart (Figure 25) is uniquely developed and mapped against each of the different thinking preference maps. Essentially, the SORT chart reflects the strengths, opportunities, resistances for growth and the techniques and ways to overcome any resistance for the child. Each person has his or her own unique SORT. The stakeholder can appropriately identify the SORT and then suggest activities and the skills aligning to overcome the resistance.

Strengths	Opportunities
Identifying the unique strengths in relation to problem-solving, communication and overall leading life.	Particular opportunities aligned to the strengths in a career field.
Resistances	Techniques (Overcoming resistances)
The resistance could be in the form of difficulty in pursuing a particular skill due to misalignment of the thinking preference.	The skills and extracurricular activities suggested to the child to help them overcome the same through a conscious understanding.

FIGURE 25. STRENGTHS AND OPPORTUNITIES OF THE SORT CHART.

The idea of the SORT chart is derived from the very popular SWOT chart used for personal and business analysis. The SORT concept focuses on the development of underutilised preferences.

No person reading this book would want to commit to an average ordinary life for themselves or their children. The extraordinary life is nothing but a mindset or a brain's thinking type. Once each person becomes aware of his or her unique brain's thinking type, navigating life and interacting with other people becomes a piece of cake.

Remember when making life decisions, it pays to be self-aware. Let us now see the seventeen different cognitive preference maps.

Cognitive Preference Maps (CPMs)

A set of seventeen different cognitive preference maps or CPMs has been developed. Each child has a unique CPM. The chronology of thinking from the most desired to least desired preferences is mapped and different maps derived. Each CPM has its own SORT.

Each map highlights the point that the brain is not watertight in its thinking preference but often has an overlay and influence from the other types.

The CPMs are segregated into four major types:
- Solo thinkers
- Dual thinkers
- Triple thinkers
- Box brains

The solo thinkers have a single quadrant or part of the brain firing all the way. These people have a unique SORT based on their types. The solo thinkers have limited support from other brain types. They are primarily driven only through the understanding of one quadrant of the brain's thinking domain. Their major strengths are only aligned to that particular type of the brain quadrant. They do not pay much attention to the other areas as they are not stimulated enough to allow them to utilise it enough in their daily life. These areas represent the resistance.

The dual thinkers have a combination of two different types of thinking.

Cognitive dual types 1 + 2: This is a combination of analytical and innovative processing.

Left-sided dual types 1 + 3: This is a combination of analytical and method-based reasoning.

Limbic dual types 3 + 4: This is a combination of method and people-based reasoning.

Right-sided dual types 2 + 4: This is a combination of innovative processing and people-based reasoning.

The cross-thinkers are unique thinkers driven by seemingly opposite quadrants or cross-quadrants of the brain.

Type I or types 1 + 4: This is a combination of analytical processing and people-based reasoning.

Type II or types 2 + 3: This is a combination of innovation-based processing and method-based reasoning. I have a classic brain profile that belongs to this category.

While the triple-thinkers have a similar pattern, their thinking is dominated by three areas of the brain.

Triple-thinker A or types 1 + 2 + 3
Triple-thinker B or types 1 + 2 + 4
Triple-thinker C or types 3 + 4 + 1
Triple-thinker D or types 3 + 4 + 2

What are Box Brains?

Last but not least are the box brains (types 1, 2, 3 and 4). These are people who are equally driven in all four quadrants. To cut out a passion or drive for a unique thing becomes easy and hard at the same time. They can pursue any task provided to them with ease. Carving a unique passion and firing towards a certain career becomes difficult. They are not so commonly found. But children who are box thinkers should be encouraged to develop a passion for one side of the brain's preference and continuously train that particular part of the brain to achieve focus and attention.

The SORT chart for the box brains is presented below (Figure 26).

Strengths	Opportunities
They can be persuaded to take up any task. They understand tasks pretty easily and can have a flair for multi-tasking. They can relate their work to the world easily and clearly. They also identify with various types of thinking pretty easily.	Particular opportunities aligned to the strengths in a career field should be provided.
Resistances	**Techniques (Overcoming resistances)**
They cannot decide clearly. They have a problem heading in a particular direction. They are often side-tracked multiple times. They have a very tight brain. Knowing and understanding others' opinions takes time.	A hawk-eye to their drivers and interests is necessary. They can be very efficient in handling multi-functional roles with ease. The sense of indecisiveness and lack of focus needs constant guidance.

FIGURE 26. SORT MAP FOR BOX BRAINS.

Let us now see the SORT maps linked to each of the thinking type maps.

Type 1 thinking: This type of thinking is primarily driven by the **analytical processing** from the frontal portions of the brain (Figure 27).

Strengths	Opportunities
Analysis	Data and informatics
Research	Research positions
Data	Academics
Detailed review	Directorship
Resistances	**Techniques/Courses**
Loss of big picture	Course in arts/design
Too much insistence on being right	Body language and emotional expression courses
Analysis-paralysis	Animation and filmmaking
Only data-based decisions	Extempore speaking

FIGURE 27. SORT MAP FOR TYPE 1 THINKING.

Type 2 thinking: This type of thinking is primarily driven by the **innovative processing** largely driven by the parieto-occipital portions of the brain (Figure 28).

Strengths	Opportunities
Big picture thinking	Entrepreneurship
Innovation	Enterprise ownership/leadership
Drive and motivation	Arts and creative careers
Risk-taking	Leadership
Resistances	**Techniques/Courses**
Analysis	Courses in programming
Detailed review	Research methodologies
Data and facts	AI/Machine learning courses
Research	Learning bridge/chess (such related games)

FIGURE 28. SORT MAP FOR TYPE 2 THINKING.

Type 3 thinking: This type is driven by **method-based reasoning**, which is driven by the frontal and partly limbic cortex of the brain (Figure 29).

Strengths	Opportunities
Detailed review	Applied sciences
Methodical analysis	Operations
Timely delivery	Organisation
Protection and safekeeping	Management
Resistances	**Techniques/Courses**
Big picture thinking	Body language processing
Innovation	Design courses
Creativity and arts	Space and landscape programs
Socialisation	Travel and culture

FIGURE 29. SORT MAP FOR TYPE 3 THINKING.

Type 4 thinking: This type is driven by **people-based reasoning**, which is largely from the limbic cortex (Figure 30).

Strengths	Opportunities
Empathy	Caring careers
Teamwork	Marketing /sales
Connections	Humanities
Support	Hospitality
Resistances	**Techniques/Courses**
Data	Coding and programming
Analysis	Designing
Method based processes	Research methodologies
Big picture thinking	AI/Machine learning

FIGURE 30. SORT MAP FOR TYPE 4 THINKING.

Master Career Cluster Chart

The master career cluster chart (Figure 31) allows us to check the major careers applicable to each thinking type. It also allows us to dissect the choices within each of the career groups.

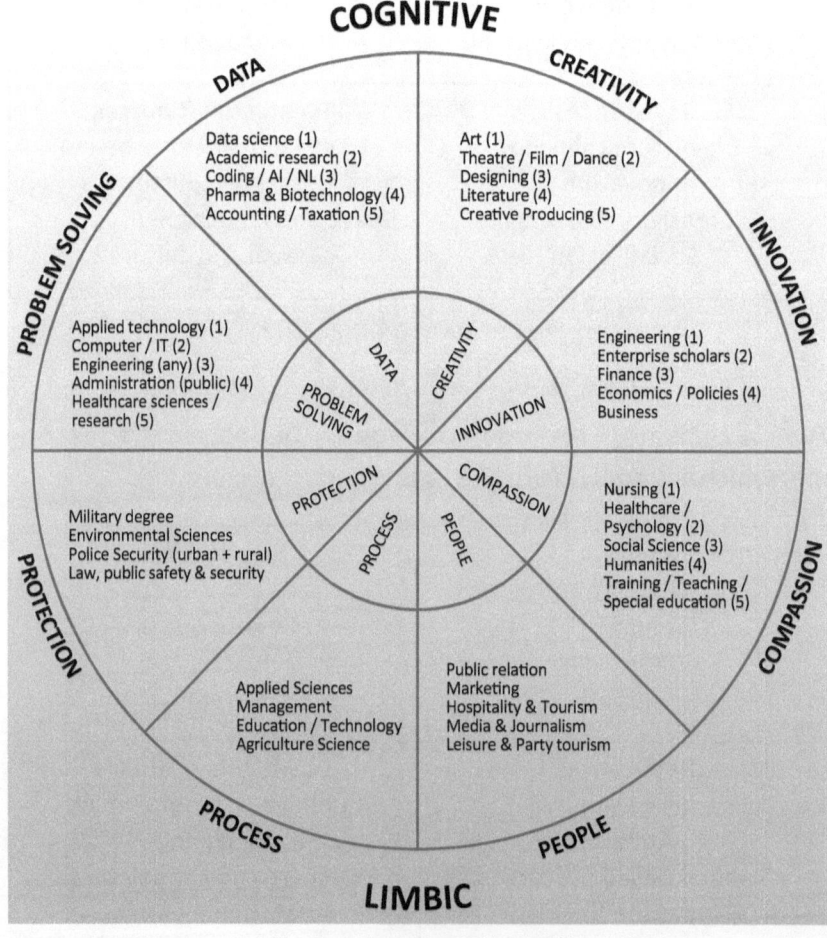

FIGURE 31. DRAWING OF THE MASTER CAREER CLUSTER CHART (IMAGE BY THE AUTHOR).

Let's take some examples to drive home the point. A child who is undergoing an assessment ends up having a dominant type 1 + 3 thinking pattern. This is the left dual pattern. For each child that we counsel we have a five-step formula that we apply. Let me enumerate the steps and you can also do this exercise later. This is simply to conjure the picture of the child's thinking pathway in our heads. This allows us to navigate the session quite smoothly.

Step 1. Identify the *Mybraindesign*® cognitive flow map. In this case, types 1 + 3 = left dual type.

Step 2. Identify the major drivers in these two thinking preferences. Highlight the drivers. Let us say in this case the drivers are data and operations.

Step 3. Pick the careers from the two first flow map derivatives. In this example, types 1 + 3.

Step 4. Pick the careers specific to the drivers for process and analysis.

Step 5. Check the interests of the child and filter the most represented career from the cluster.

By allowing yourself to map out the five steps you will end up identifying the top careers relating to types 1 + 3 thinking. For this example, in particular, the careers would be data sciences, applied sciences, and technology-based roles.

The final choice would be based upon drawing a *lifedesign* print.

To solidify the technique further, let me provide an example from one of my former students. I had a student named Aaron who was confused about his career choice. He was a type 1 and type 2 thinker. He was clearly a cognitive upper or rational brain. He had finished his Bachelor of Computing but had no clue about his next move. He did not enjoy computer coding very much and became an engineer but there was no spark of joy in learning coding. In fact, he indicated that he enjoyed graphic design, which was offered for a month during his entire computer engineering career. While he was strongly data and innovation-driven, it was clear that coding was not his desired career choice.

A typical engineer in computers would have been comfortable if he was a type 1 and type 3 left dual-thinker. The people with left dual-thinking patterns are quite comfortable with technical tasks. They do not have the urge or drive to innovate or create new things. They are quite happy following the orders of their superiors. While Aaron was sure that he could not follow orders, he did not want to work in a setting where his ideas were not heard. He was at a very critical juncture where he had spent two years only thinking about his next move.

A very clear career path was imminent once the cluster was laid. This thinking profile is highly suited to an entrepreneur or management consultant. His next bet could be to pursue an MBA in IT/systems or finance by completely pivoting from computer engineering. I suggested this to him and he is now working with one of the top four management consultants in finance.

I want you to work around the exercises and try to find the best career choices for the students. Let me give you simple problems to solve.
- Try to design the careers for a child who is a type 1 + 4 contrast dual-thinker
- Try to design the careers for a child who is a type 2 + 4 right dual-thinker

Never underestimate the drivers of thinking. It is important to check for the drivers, the various indices, interests, academic strengths, and other factors such as family background, financial factors, and available resources before you provide the final career advice (Figure 32). The above exercises are simply provided to strengthen the concept of *Mybraindesign*®.

Drivers of the Brain

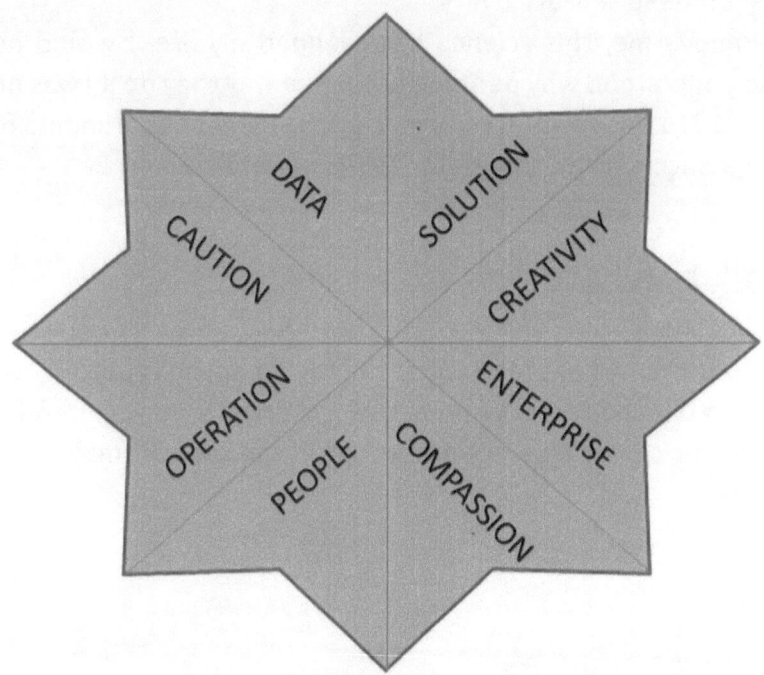

FIGURE 32. DRAWING OF THE BRAIN DRIVERS (IMAGE BY THE AUTHOR).

Conditions to Success

This chapter has highlighted how easily one can refine the career choice based on the type of thinking pattern. Taking an informed decision using a scientific tool is important. Now let us draw out the *lifedesign* print for the child. We need to factor in all the above details before we come to a near-final conclusion for the career choice.

It is helpful to go through the details one more time before you go to the next step. The fundamental game of career success is indeed self-discovery.

Believe me, this science has changed my life. I would not have understood why people behave the way they do if I was not exposed to this science. I could do all the career experiments for myself successfully, thanks to *Mybraindesign*®.

Walk the talk

Map out the careers for each of the four thinking types.

Map out the careers for each of the drivers. You can refer to the minor career clusters presented in the drivers' map in the chapter.

9

Let's Live By Purpose, and Not By Accident

Your *Lifedesign Blueprint*®: Summing Up the Journey to a Clear Future by Integrating the Ingredients to the Right Career Choice

'A clear vision backed by definite plans, gives you a tremendous feeling of confidence and personal power.'

— BRIAN TRACY

Allowing No Happenstance

This very well-expressed quote that is on the Rindge School of Technical Arts in Cambridge, Massachusetts, summarises the efforts of the book: 'Work is one of our greatest blessings. Everyone should have an honest occupation.' The honest occupation is nothing but what is aligned to our thinking preferences, interests, skills, and most importantly, our fundamental existence and meaning in life.

Each person on the planet is seeking to discover their meaning in life. The 'A-ha!' moment of career success is a process. The *lifedesign blueprint*® sums up the entire process of career discovery as described in the book.

The students have a collection of attributes and skills with a constant focus on the ability to learn continuously. If career planning is done in an efficient manner, the students would at the very least be following the career plan of informed decision-making, rather than one of the happenstances.

Simple Yet Powerful Outcome-Based Formula

This *lifedesign blueprint*® is developed by keeping the total process and progress of the career journey in mind. It is designed to explore all the relevant internal and external factors influencing career choices. It is designed as a simple visual display graph on which the details can be plotted and relevant decisions about extracurricular activities, choices, subjects, curriculum choices, and further career path choices are mapped.

The three frames of the *lifedesign* allow us to plot all the essential details about the career path discovery. The decision about the best career choice, the skills necessary to be updated and upgraded, and consideration of all the other necessary resources shall be clarified.

Thanks to the wonders of neuroplasticity, adolescents are primed to improve their performance in school and beyond.

Clarity Breeds Focus for the Career Path

Neuroscience has time and again stressed the point that clarity allows the brain to focus on the tasks at hand without any distractions. Goal-setting exercises are essentially very important so that the rational and emotional brains can work in synchronicity. Both will keep the other focused on moving towards the situations and behaviours that lead to the achievement of the goal and ignoring the situations and behaviours that are not helping. The goal-setting literally changes the structure of the brain so that it is optimised to achieve the goal.

I wish I had the same process available for me in high school. I probably would have been a full-time creator or innovator. The moment I plotted my life on the blueprint, it was clear that I had to acquire the skills for management, and I decided to work hard towards it. I could go through the rigor of the GMAT entrance exam despite being a biology student all my life and then start to build micro-ventures proving the point that I can be accepted by the top schools in the world.

Without the help of the right process and the vision board helping to plot my own goals for career progression, I could not have done what I have achieved in life. This book is also essentially an inspiration as plotted on the *lifedesign* matrix.

The Inspiration of the Blueprint

The idea of the *lifedesign blueprint*® is borrowed from a fellow Cambridge alumnus, Songya Kesler, who designed the life canvas.

The *lifedesign blueprint*® is a three-factor model. Figure 34 illustrates the blueprint. The central frame showcases the intersection of interest-based careers and brain-design-derived career clusters. The other two frames showcase the internal and external factors.

The inner frame focuses on the available resources in the school or home options to have extra-curricular skills, the focused subjects offered in the schools, and the curriculum offered in the school.

The outer frame focuses on the financial resources, the family commitment, and most importantly the availability of the career/course in the subject's country. This would also mean plotting the need to travel to another country or place to find a career if necessary.

The final choice of the career would take into consideration the inner and outer frame characteristics and match it to the common careers identified in the central frame.

The Central Frame: Focusing on the Interests, Cognitive Flow Map and the Skills of the Child

The central frame highlights the interests of the child and the careers extrapolated from those interests. While the upper part has the macro-career clusters plotted from the results of the brain-design test, the bottom frame highlights the micro-cluster careers.

LET'S LIVE BY PURPOSE, AND NOT BY ACCIDENT

We discussed the point earlier in the book that planning the career path and trajectory merely based on a potential interest fad could be disastrous. While some students hold on to their interests for a long period of time from adolescence until adulthood, most have difficulty in keeping those interests alive for long. For students, the motivation behind their interests is often always external. Hence, one should focus on interests but allow the clusters to be highlighted in the central frame.

Learning about *lifedesign* should not be a one-way exercise. The children must be a part of the whole process. In our experience, by conducting the bootcamps in many countries and over many years, we have realised that children grasp all the concepts much better than adults.

1-Academic capabilities 2-Available course and subject options at the school 3- Available extra-curricular options at the school/extra hours at home	Map careers offered based on *Mybraindesign*® career cluster map	1) Explore financial options 2) Family background/genetic influence/available resources
	Identify interest-based career options and map here	
	Identify the common careers from the intersection as above and highlight here.	3) Opportunity to travel outside the city/country

FIGURE 33. DIAGRAM OF THE *LIFEDESIGN BLUEPRINT*®
(DIAGRAM BY THE AUTHOR).

Sir Ebrall's tip ...

Learning involves three key components of the brain – neurons, synapses, and myelin. Neurons are nerve cells in the brain that branch to receive signals. The space separating the wire of one neuron from another is called a synapse. Learning happens when experiences connect the neurons together. Repeated practice guided by feedback helps the neurons fire better with the laying of the cover myelin which can then consolidate the learning.

Smart brains are efficient brains, and that efficiency comes from myelinating brain wires through repeated practice with specific feedback. Figure 34 showcases the neurons with the myelin sheath and the synapse.

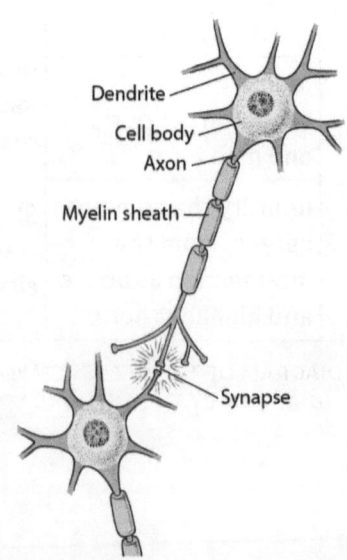

FIGURE 34. IMAGE OF NEURONS WITH MYELIN SHEATH AND SYNAPSE (IMAGE BY THE AUTHOR).

The Factors in the Frame: The Obvious and Not So Obvious

Children study in different types of schools and the available resources, courses, curriculums, and subjects can vary. One has to consider all these factors when designing the right career path. There is no one-size-fits-all approach but there is one formula that allows us to capture all the prudent factors in the frames of discovery. The factors can be further sub-divided into modifiable and non-modifiable factors. The inner frame showcases the most modifiable factors while the outer frame exhibits the most non-modifiable. The modifiable factors are ones such as extracurricular activities, courses, curriculum, and schooling, while the non-modified are ones such as finances available for the career and potential limitations in changing the country of residence.

The immediate environment for the child is a very important part in the decision-making process. The home environment, siblings, parents, and family all have an important influence on the decisions for a career.

A study has shown that parental influence on young people's career preferences is mediated by the quality of the parent-offspring relationship. The thesis has shown that family significantly influences the student's career decision-making. (1)

A famous social learning theory is based on the idea that the development of career interests is the result of an infinite number of learning experiences. What we observe from the environment in which we are surrounded offers experiences that develop into general observations and personal beliefs. Friends and peer groups are important for individual socialisation and behavioural modification. Often the influences extending from the same age group are profound.

Beyond the Obvious

Even beyond the immediate environment, the political, social, and economic issues facing the surrounding city, country, or world as a whole, determine and influence the choices of careers. One needs to carefully understand all these factors as the plotting of the matrix is done.

Let me give a very prudent example of gender and how it subtly influences career decisions. If you carefully observe the world of work, which claims that it offers equal opportunities to boys and girls, the skew in the choices is evident. The boys are still being steered towards the typical 'male'-type jobs while the girls are still expected to cluster into the traditional fields of cosmetology, teaching, psychology, and so on.

Each country is unique in its own way in regard to these not so obvious factors and teachers or parents play an important role in highlighting these factors to the children as they embark on this journey to find the best career for life.

The Next Step

Once you have plotted the map, a very clear idea about the career path, the skills necessary to boost the path, and the resources taken to achieve that path shall emerge. There may be a few careers under consideration and the priority can be based on the level of interests that the child possesses.

Plan the Extracurricular Activities Aligning with the Brain Design Map

Parents are often proud that their children are exposed to karate, music, painting, rock climbing, and swimming and that they do not have time to breathe. In reality, is this really helping the child? Planning extracurricular activities is necessary. The busy organised activity schedule can put considerable strain on the parent's resources and family relationships, as well as potentially harm the children's development and wellbeing. This was shown in a study emerging from the UK. (2)

Concept of Flow and Grow

Hobby crafting and prioritising the needs of the child are necessary. The child can do one activity in the flow section where his or her brain's preferences are aligned while the other two activities should be directed at developing the other cognitive dimensions of the brain. The idea is to not overwhelm the brain but allow it to build the right pathways and neuronal circuits to help the child. The next chapter highlights a lot of examples about flow and grow activities mapped to the types of thinking

Spending 90,000 Hours Doing What You Like is Important

We all spent about a third of our life, which is roughly 90,000 hours, working. And we know this is the longest amount of time spent each day on a task. Helping the child to have a clear focus and goal on his or her career and removing all the confusion and conflict should be the goal of any parent or teacher.

If one follows the steps as prescribed in the book, I see no reason to worry about designing the right path for our children. The entire pyramid of discovery, the *Mybraindesign*® evaluation, and the *lifedesign blueprint*® have been applied to thousands of students worldwide. If the correct steps are followed, each child's vision and mission would be as clear as water.

I believe by doing this part efficiently we are not just helping one child or family, we are contributing to the nation and world at large. Remember, we will have about two billion young children to help by the year 2025. Let us join hands in this task and remember to do it scientifically by bringing the relevant neuroscience concepts.

For me, crafting each life's dreams to their full potential is like bliss supreme. While I am sure this would be the feeling of each of the stakeholders involved in the career-path discovery process for the child. Let us see more of the flow and grow activities that we can offer to our children. Some of it can also be applicable to us.

Walk the Talk

1. Can you identify the interests of your child by observing their daily activities and play?
2. Can you draw the *lifedesign blueprint*® factors? The central frame clusters can be derived after doing an online assessment, which can be accessed at www.Mybraindesign®.org
3. Elaborate on the flow and grow activities beyond those mentioned in the chapter. After knowing your child's thinking

types, make a flow and grow chart and map the right activities for your child or student.

References

1. Mtemieri, J. (2017). *Factors influencing the choice of career pathways among high school students in Midlands Province, Zimbabwe* [Unpublished doctoral dissertation]. University of South Africa.
2. Wheeler, S. & Green, K. (2019). *Sport, Education and Society, 24*(8), 788–800.

10
Flow and Grow: Stretching the Thinking through New Hobbies and Activities

Designing Hobbies and Extracurricular Skills for Children Should Not Occur Merely to Their Choosing or Through Random Availability, but By a Dedicated and Planned Neuroscience-Based Intervention

'You are what you think all day long.'

— RALPH WALDO EMERSON

Is *Mybraindesign®* consolidated and solidified for life? If my child is a dual-cognitive-mode thinker, will he or she remain the same all their life? Or will the brain change? Can I train the brain to change? Can we influence or change our preferences? A lot of these types of questions are raised by the stakeholders when we run our training sessions.

Here's what I tell them: Brain researchers agree that individual differences in behaviour result, at least in part, from genetically determined differences in the brain. However, parenting, teaching, life experience, and cultural influences contribute far more than genetic inheritance.

Once we identify the patterns of thinking at an early age, we can start to boost the not-so-used cognitive preferences through various interventions. It is easy to develop competencies and skills in a preferred cognitive mode. However, going to the other side is like riding a boat against the river current. This requires a lot of effort and resilience.

Neuroplasticity is repeatedly referred to in this book, hence, it is always possible to grow the circuits in the not-so-preferred cognitive preferences. But you have to understand how much of it is required and to what extent the time permits.

This chapter highlights our suggestions for building the not-so-preferred areas of the brain. We have been practising the concept of flow and grow in the brain. One has to flow in the top brain preferences while one has to learn to at least get exposed and start to develop somewhat of an interest in the other not-so-utilised preference. Yes, the flow is easy, and the grow will require a lot of mental effort both by the child and also the parents, teachers, and caregivers. Finally, it is the extra mile that you walk that leads you to greener pastures.

Are We Really 'Brained'?

Ned Herrmann, the founder of the Herrmann dominance brain instruments, proposed somewhat of a hardwiring of the neural circuits in relation to the preferences. He narrated that we are 'handed', 'footed', 'eyed', 'eared' and, in a general sense, 'brained'. (1) We are all wired in a particular way for a reason. Our childhood has shaped our destiny. The first five years of childhood play a crucial role in determining the personality and the cognitive preferences of the individual. This is a clear and well-known fact in science. Each of us is created whole which means that we have the power to utilise all the portions of the brain and develop any kind of competencies as necessary.

However, what stops us from allowing all the areas of the brain to be utilised efficiently is *brain inertia*. Brain inertia is interesting and even we, as adults, are victims of it.

One expert claims that the mind works to recognise familiar patterns and likes to follow only the already known route. This actually then makes further thinking unnecessary. To get more comfortable shifting, it's helpful to practice shifting into a particular mode in the context of something you love. Shifting is not easy but once learned at an early age, it pays till late. (2)

Shifting the Brain Sets

Let us take the example of driving a car. The moment you find a route known to you, you do not need to use a map or compass or ask for directions. Finding your way happens without really thinking about it. In a way, our thinking is an ongoing search for these familiar roads that make thinking unnecessary. A pattern is a repeatable sequence of neural activities. In practice, a pattern is any repeatable concept, idea, thought, or image. There is no limit to the size of the pattern and the only requirements are that a pattern should be repeatable, recognisable, and usable.

The four brain preferences/pillars of *Mybraindesign*® can be seen as an organising principle for all our thinking preferences into a sensible whole. But the moment we are comfortable in a set pattern, we start avoiding or rejecting other approaches. For an analytical or fact-driven child, intuition is suspect, while for an intuitive or enterprise-driven child factual data is boring and distracting. The people-driven person cannot be driven by the process if not nudged appropriately.

Default Thinking Mode and Autopilot Life

According to Professor Ned Herrmann, the stronger our preference for one way of thinking, the stronger our discomfort with the opposite mode will be. People functioning in opposite modes have great difficulty in communicating with and understanding each other because they see the world through different eyes or filters (patterns).

I am a classical example of this phenomenon. I am a low people-driven driver. I made it a point to make sure that I practised talking to my patients and clients daily. I started to enjoy the process and slowly over time, I developed competency in this area. I can now easily communicate and, in fact, also drive home a point to an audience because I have developed the competency consciously.

However, here is the catch. In my free time and leisure, I will go back to the dominant innovative thinking mode that I possess followed by methodical reasoning. My brain is just happy being there. It enjoys the autopilot mode. I can have creative ideas like flowing juice. I can work on any project that is innovative for days and months long. I get attracted to anything that is risky and out rightly tough. This is all because of my default thinking process.

It is like wearing nice formal wear going to a party and as soon as you are back home, you go back to your pyjamas. We are always comfortable in the repetitive pattern of thinking. The brain wants to conserve energy. The autopilot mode is *real*.

Sir Ebrall's view ...

Our autopilot mode seems to be run by a set of brain structures called the default mode network (DMN). The DMN was realised in the 1990s when researchers noticed that people lying in brain scanners show patterns of brain activity even when they aren't really doing anything. This research provided the first evidence that our brains are active even when we aren't consciously putting our minds to work.

But what does the DMN do? Several studies have found that it seems to be involved in assessing past events and planning for the future. Others suggest that the network is involved in self-awareness, although this has been called into question by findings that rats and newborns appear to have a version of the DMN, too.

The idea is that the autopilot mode actually allows us to better focus on tasks or actually takes away from the potential of doing new tasks? Lots of experiments are being conducted in this regard. In fact, through neurofeedback techniques, one can strengthen the DMN allowing the person to perform better at all tasks. We allow children to run some programs in our experience centre with neurofeedback. The results are great to see. They can learn better, focus better, have a calm and engaging attitude, and can also express themselves better.

Why Does the Brain Resist Doing New Things?

Currently, at the time of writing, we are in the midst of the Covid-19 pandemic. We as adults are also constantly running multiple errands to make sure we sail the rough time. A mother is multitasking and so is the father. The teachers are adopting hybrid learning models.

The times we feel like this, our brains want to save mental energy by directing our focus to the most readily available, recallable information to help us make decisions in a jiffy. We often do this by going with our gut and making our best guess. This is called expediency bias: doing the thing that feels right, or rushing to judgment, without properly considering all the variables. The brain does this because it's much easier to process existing ideas than new ones, a principle in psychology called fluency.

The Hedonic principle also comes into play: We are wired to move toward things that make us feel good and away from things that make us feel uncomfortable. Our brains tag effort as bad because it's hard work.

They default to what feels 'normal' – the networks that tell us where and how to navigate through our daily life. Those networks are so deep in our thinking that when we're travelling a new and challenging path – regardless of what that path is – our wheels default back to the worn-in grooves. (3)

The bottom line is that yes, allowing the children to develop the not-so-developed thinking mode is going to be a tough game. But the point to drive home is that doing this early and in a timely manner is the magical pill to swallow.

Doing it in a Timely Manner and Doing it Right is important: Overcoming Brain Inertia

There are two fundamental ways we can allow our children to be exposed to both halves of the brain. One is designing their hobbies and the second is allowing them to pursue some short courses before they join their careers. We also have a well-planned career experience routine set up for the kids for this purpose in our programs. This allows them to understand what kind of activity is best suited for overcoming brain inertia. The biceps muscles do not grow by merely talking to them to grow. We need to take conscious efforts in our daily lives to allow for growth in a particular direction.

Balance is the Key

It is important that we do not overwhelm the children's circuits but allow them to choose what they like. Chronic underlying stress has been shown to work like acid for the hypothalamus. It can damage the brain. The stress of performance and time pressure can harm the growth of young brains and studies have shown that it can stunt brain growth. Doing more is better for the brain but overdoing it is essentially killing the brain.

It is necessary that we craft the tasks delicately, striking a balance in time and effort where we are doing enough to overcome inertia but not too much. At best, two activities promoting the flow part and one for the grow part are all that is prescribed. Once the children pick up a particular skill-building course, we should be monitoring them. We should not allow them to stop it prematurely. There is a tendency for the children to overreact to their moods or interests. We should play the role of coaches and slowly nudge the children to complete those activities. It is in their great favour that we are doing the task often of a police officer.

Let me give you some distinct examples of how you can design the hobbies and also the courses that can allow the growth of the various types of thinking for the children. You can choose any of the activities based on the interests, availability, and financial reach of the family. There is no hard and fast rule when it comes to the quadrant choices. Yes, it is important to be careful to keep the flow and grow concept intact as one decides to pursue the activities.

Stretching the Thinking through Hobbies

Analytical processing	Innovative processing
Billiards	Applied arts
Golf	Creative writing
Number puzzles	Video games
Statistics	Multimedia
Computer programming	Photography
Model building	Dance
DIY games	Poems/literature

Method-based reasoning	People-based reasoning
Baking	Travel
Fishing	Theatre
Gardening	Social services
Bodybuilding	Fiction-based reading
Collecting	Team sports
Bridge/chess	History and museum visits

Stretching Through Opting for Various Extracurricular Activities/Courses

Computer programming Coding Big data analysis Machine learning Statistics Research	Landscaping and space design Web and other designing Multimedia Innovation and start-up Theatre and studio
Technological courses Robotics Engineering courses Courses in AI Repair	Communication and speaking clubs UN model courses Cultural influences Travel and tourism Volunteering First aid courses

Stretching Through Small, Daily Practices

Making a 'to do' list Making a timetable overview for exams No mobile, television or social media for a week	Going out to fun places unplanned Mind-mapping the lessons Learning a new musical instrument
Journalising Rearranging the closet Taking detailed notes in class	Making five new friends Going to an NGO Social media interaction with a completely new set of friends across different countries

The Role of Unconscious Processes in Learning

Human learning is manifested through multidimensional and interacting perceptual, cognitive, and emotional processes. Any kind of learning is unlikely to occur effectively without the interaction between prior knowledge and cognitive abilities, and the emotional and motivational states of learners. Learning processes must have an unconscious, implicit, unintentional, intuitive, automatic processing stage mainly because of the limited conscious processing ability of the brain. The unconscious promptly works on the information patterns through the environmental stimulus. **(4)**

To be able to make a lasting impact on the thinking of children, it is important for us to work together with them by helping to facilitate the growth of the brain. We, as the children's stakeholders, should also be aware of our brain design and allow us to sink to their needs. Assigning them to particular hobbies and courses is easy. The difficult part is allowing them to be sensitive to the environment and making them subconsciously learn in the environment.

A small matrix is presented here as Figure 35, which allows parents and teachers to subconsciously process the needs of the children. The matrix allows them to build the right type of environment at school and home.

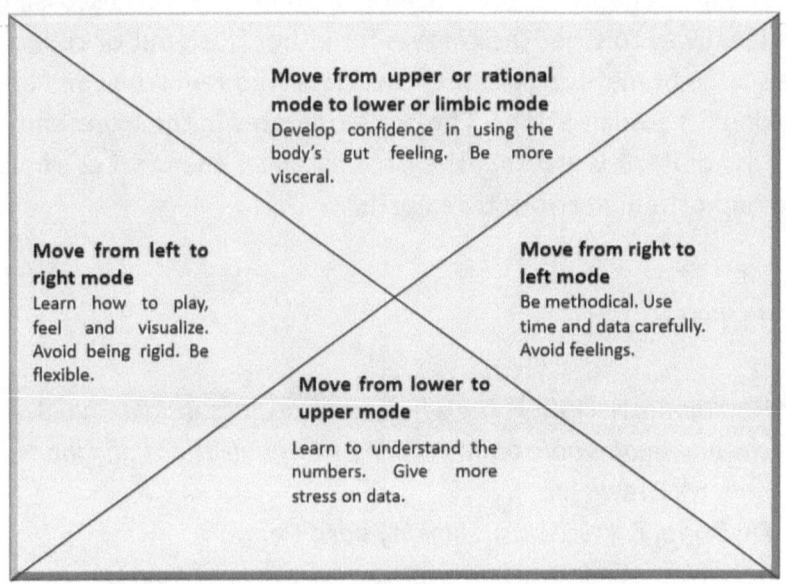

FIGURE 35. MATRIX OUTLINING THE SHIFTS OF LEARNING (DIAGRAM BY THE AUTHOR).

Doing things that feel uncomfortable and like hard work can seem counterintuitive. But by understanding what's going on in the brain, instead of the gut, one can work towards accomplishing hard things and most importantly allow the children to develop all the areas of the brain with ease. This will allow them to be not just accomplished but also successful in life.

This is Just the Beginning and Not an End

This chapter has demystified the process of flow and grow and has also summarised activities promoting the not-so-preferred brain preferences of the child. I am sure many of you may be wondering, while this process sounds great for young children, what about the adults who are stuck in their choices and who feel stifled in their chosen careers or jobs?

The next chapter is presented as a bonus chapter discussing the ideal way to steer the careers for either fresh out of college graduates or mid-life career enthusiasts who feel stuck and are looking for some options. The brain operates in the exact same way as adults. It is just that the circumstances change. Let's help you find or validate your true north.

References

1. Herrmann, N. (1996). *The whole brain business book: Unlocking the power of whole brain thinking in organizations and individuals*. McGraw-Hill.
2. De Bono, E. (1981). *Six thinking hats*. Penguin.
3. See https://hbr.org/2021/12/how-to-convince-yourself-to-do-hard-things
4. Moreno, R. (2010) Cognitive load theory: More food for thought. *Instructional Science, 38*, 135–141. https://doi.org/10.1007/s11251-009-9122-9

11

Adult Bonus Chapter

Finding the True North for You

'If you don't like how things are, change it! You are not a tree.'

— JIM ROHN

'If you don't build your dream, someone will hire you to build their dreams.'

— TONY GASKINS

A global poll conducted by Gallup has uncovered that only 15% of the world's one billion full-time workers consider themselves engaged at work. That means that an astronomical 85% of people are unhappy in their jobs. When topics such as work-life balance, employee engagement, and company culture seem to be as hot in the press as they currently are, it's almost impossible to fathom why this percentage is so high.

On average, we spend around a third of our lives at work. That's around 90,000 waking hours across an average lifetime. How many times have you heard about people who end up sick, depressed, divorced, abusing substances, etc., because they're unhappy with their careers? What if they liked their careers instead? Couldn't helping them navigate to the right space have a huge impact on the health and welfare of society?

Finding a career path that makes us feel happy and successful is never easy. It is not something that is ever taught systematically in school. There is no formal guidance available on career path navigation after college. Post-college adults are rarely asked if they feel comfortable in their chosen path.

The post-college graduate has lots to think about in terms of earning, family, work-life balance, hobbies, and progress and he/she ends up in this love-hate relationship cycle. He loves that he has a job because of the career choice but hates that the job is only earning him a meagre salary but not really making him happy or fulfilled. I don't say this applies to the majority. But this is quite a common problem that we encounter.

We undertook a telephonic survey asking respondents about career fulfilment and the type of work they were doing. The answers were eye-opening. The majority of people in our survey were not doing jobs related or only somewhat related to their careers and most were hanging on because of the salaries.

I have a ton of friends who are misfits in their proposed careers as chartered accountants, doctors, lawyers, or engineers. I have also met people who have developed the courage to change their path completely and not conform to the earning parameters. What is driving them to undertake such a radical change? How can insights of self-discovery coupled with a clear steering path help them re-shift to the careers they want in life?

Let us focus on how you can rethink the choices for a career even at a later stage in life. Oftentimes, a person can start experimenting with other career choices as a side hustle and slowly move full-time once enough know-how is gained. The tool *Mybraindesign*® helps to guide adults in various stages of their career or work lifecycles. It is not restricted to high school students. Our research team has performed a separate statistical validation for the tools that apply to post-college adults.

Career Decisions are Always Tricky

Every career has its wrong turns, and some have more than others. At the midlife point, we find ourselves reflecting ruefully on what might have been. A friend of mine gave up a promising career in dance to become a doctor. Ten years in, she found her work disappointingly drab. What haunted her was not so much wondering how to change tracks now but wishing she could change the past. Why had she made the mistake of giving up on the career that she loved? How could she make peace with that?

As the spiritualist, Robert Adams, wrote, 'If our lives are good, we have reason to be glad we have had them rather than lives that would have been even better but too thoroughly different.'

When I think I should have been a finance expert or an entrepreneur, not a doctor, and begin to regret my choice, I am ignoring the texture of my work and the countless ways in which the value of what I am doing is made vivid to me as I do it – i.e., in a patient's life, in a student's lives through the research, or in the world at large because of the scale of the work in health and education that I can offer. I would never have been able to do this as a finance expert. Indeed, it is the specifics that count against the grand cartoon of lives unlived.

The Mid-Life Career Crisis is the Worst

An abundance of recent research confirms that middle age is, on average, the most difficult time of life. In 2008, economists David Blanchflower and Andrew Oswald found that self-reported life satisfaction takes the form of a gently curving 'U', beginning high in youth, bottoming out in our mid-forties, and then recovering as we get older. The pattern is robust around the world, affecting both men and women. And it persists when we correct for other variables, such as parenthood. (1)

For me, the deepest source of malaise at the point of mid-career was not regretting the past but a sense of futility in the present. My work still seemed worthwhile: I saw value in treating patients, researching, and writing. Yet there was something hollow in life that loomed ahead. That is when I decided to step up and upskill myself by doing an MBA from Cambridge. This changed my life.

Although daunting at the age of thirty-eight to do a full-time rigorous and hectic program in business, it was the most fulfilling decision of my life. Finally, a lease of fresh air enveloped me as I completed the course. I could roll up my sleeves and undertake finance, enterprise projects, writing books, coaching programs, analysing stocks, business, investing, and much more. I would have never fathomed doing this being a physician.

The ego identity theory of Joan Erikson exclaims that during adulthood, we continue to build our lives, focusing on our careers and family. (2) Those who are successful during this phase will feel that they are contributing to the world by being active in their home and community. Those who fail to attain this skill will feel unproductive and uninvolved in the world.

Developing a Mindset That Fosters Success

Having experienced an explosion in personal development, success coaching, and lifestyle engineering, today's world has never been hungrier for the glory of goal achievement. Whether these goals stem from desires for fitness, entrepreneurship or some other domain, they all have one thing in common – a road paved with uncertainty, sacrifice, and setbacks. As such, it is key that you learn to foster a sense of resilience within yourself to ensure you overcome these setbacks to aid your rise to greatness.

Honest Self-Check

How many times have you found success in the eyes of others but lacked inner joy or satisfaction within yourself? Is there a way to crack the success code and build a career (and a life) that satisfies your deepest values and also fulfils your definition of success in this world?

The Total Magic of Life is Summarised in One Word: 'Consonance'

Consonance, as exclaimed by Laura Gassner Otting, happens when what you do matches who you are. Achieving consonance, however, is not for the weak-willed. (3) It is hard to achieve and requires deep thinking and re-analysis of your own strengths and opportunities. The process is no different from the self-discovery analysis we have looked at for the children. The career pyramid for success still holds true. The steps are pretty much the same. Awareness of the various virtual tools for job and career courses is necessary. Dedicating a self-inquiry routine and performing authentic research for changing your career path or job is required.

It is Too Never Late For a Self-discovery Analysis

If you are feeling stuck and relate to the chapter's discussion, please allow yourself to opt for the self-discovery assessment. The same assessment discussed in previous chapters applies also to adults with a different set of questions, of course. The science backing *Mybraindesign*® is no different.

Feeling Stuck is Healthy, Not Doing Anything About it is Unhealthy

Are you the one who is thinking about quitting your job one minute and then wondering the next minute whether you should just stay put? You are applying for jobs but secretly you feel you cannot be hanging on in the same career. The present job or career is like a boulder pass that you cannot cross. Stuck is nothing but a very superficial feeling in the brain. The deeper connections of emotions are required to be unfolded. Getting to know your authentic and true self is necessary. Spending time knowing your strengths is required.

Remember what is elucidated by neuroscience – **clarity comes from actions, not thoughts.** You can't think your way into clarity. You cannot imagine one fine day I am going to wake up and feel unstuck, it never works. You have to act. Actions result in feedback. Your analysis will allow you to know yourself better. The feedback provides clarity and clarity brings confidence. You are always in control of your career, and it is your responsibility to change the course of your career if you are stuck or unhappy.

Not Giving Up is the Key

There are ample stories of not giving up. The most famous one is that of Colonel Sanders. You got it right. He is the guy whose recipe was rejected over a thousand times before anyone accepted it.

It wasn't until age forty that he began selling chicken dishes in a service station. As he began to advertise his food, an argument with a competitor resulted in a deadly shootout. Four years later, he bought a motel that burned to the ground along with his restaurant. Yet this determined man rebuilt and ran a new motel until World War II forced him to close it down.

Sander's 'secret recipe' was coined Kentucky Fried Chicken. After years of failures and misfortunes, Sanders finally hit it big. At age ninety, Sanders passed away from pneumonia. At that time, there were around 6,000 KFC locations in forty-eight countries. By 2013, there were an estimated 18,000 KFC locations in 118 countries.

If you're overwhelmed by rejection or discouraged by setbacks, remember the story of Colonel Harland Sanders. Fired from multiple jobs, a ruined legal career, and a range of other setbacks including the Great Depression, fires, and World War II, yet still able to create one of the largest fast-food chains in the world. Sanders wouldn't let anything or anyone defeat him.

Let us see how the pyramid of career success applies to adults (Figure 36). It is essentially the exact same pyramid that we learned for our children. You can advance level by level by mapping the activities so that you can achieve the top of the career success.

FIGURE 36. THE PYRAMID OF CAREER SUCCESS (IMAGE BY THE AUTHOR).

How Decision-Making is Necessary to be Understood

Who is actually in charge when we make decisions in daily life? Individual decisions are best understood as the interactions between deliberation and impulse. Nobel laureate Daniel Kahneman has described these two systems as *deliberative* (**System 2**) and *impulsive* (**System 1**) (see Figure 37). The deliberative system is typically effortful. When we are calm, the deliberative system guides slow rational thinking. **(4)**

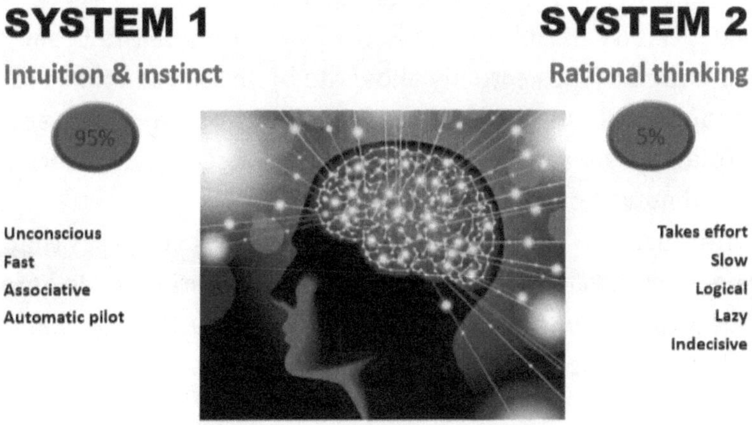

SYSTEM 1
Intuition & instinct

95%

Unconscious
Fast
Associative
Automatic pilot

SYSTEM 2
Rational thinking

5%

Takes effort
Slow
Logical
Lazy
Indecisive

FIGURE 37. KAHNEMAN'S *IMPULSIVE* AND *DELIBERATIVE* SYSTEMS (IMAGE RECREATED FROM *THINKING, FAST AND SLOW*)

The impulsive system acts spontaneously without consideration for the broader consequences of the action. The everyday snap judgments are made by the impulsive system without processing information. The impulsive system is relatively effortless and spontaneous.

The final decision is determined based on the relative strength of the impulsive system and the deliberative system.

The ability to 'balance' these two systems is critical for successful self-control and sustaining effortful control in pursuit of long-term goals. Self-control failure implies that these two systems come into conflict with each other.

Old Habits Die Hard

The psychologist Gerald Edelman noted that most of our habits take shape at the neural level through the connections between brain cells. The more often a particular circuit in the brain is used, the stronger its connections become. **(5)**

Old habits definitely die hard. The wiring of the brain is so hard-coded that to actually allow the brain to break that pattern is a tough call. Insight is never enough for a change. It needs to be followed by repeated efforts to reinforce new understanding and new coping skills.

Research on the power of neuroplasticity suggests that the brain is actually malleable and shaped by experience. No amount of pep talk or understanding would actually lead to making a shift and change. It is the continuous efforts and real action that make the change.

Rethinking Life

If you are in middle age and wondering if it is too late to think about a career or life decision. Or if you are thinking about what your spouse or child would say. Let me clarify this for you, straight up. You're in your 40s, and the only person whose opinion matters is your own!

According to a study, 82% of adults forty-seven and older who attempted a career change after the age of forty-five were ultimately successful. The key is to recognise that you are not just reinventing your career. You are also redefining yourself as a human being because the process starts from the inside out.

Shifting From Head to Heart is Necessary

It is necessary that you let go of the limiting beliefs and follow the appropriate self-discovery process. You want to know what brings joy and happiness to you. You want to face your authentic and true self.

It is necessary to engage in the opportunity awareness exercise that allows you to explore ample avenues to expand your options. Many online portals are matching your talents and interests or skills to the organisations. It is important to spend time learning the latest online resources allowing you to take a leap from your existing career to the one you have always desired.

No matter your age, it's wise to embrace social media. The benefit of curating your online presence is that it can help you further your reach and expand your network. At the very least, you should have a robust LinkedIn profile that reflects the 'new' you. Ensure that you control the message that you put out to the world rather than leaving it to chance. Trend surfing is the key. Being aware of the various career trends is necessary. Merely operating from fear that catching up with the latest trends is difficult and is not going to do the job.

As motivational speaker Michael Altshuler said, 'The bad news is time flies. The good news is you're the pilot.' So, chart your course, buckle up, and prepare for take-off.

Expanding the Career Advancement Opportunities

Online upskilling options are plenty. There is a ton of websites allowing you to take courses and certification programs, which can be of great assistance to people requiring help to expand their opportunity awareness and their career consciousness. LinkedIn is a great resource. There are many open universities online. Other good resources are:
1. Codecademy
2. FutureLearn
3. ALISON
4. Udemy
5. Coursera
6. edX
7. Udacity
8. LinkedIn Learning
9. Skillshare

One should first make a crystalised plan about how to navigate to the right choice and then reach out online to the right people who can guide you further in establishing the path ahead. Furthermore, one should always be keeping the *lifedesign blueprint*® in mind, including the internal and external factors pertaining to finances and family so that the priority can be accurately established. The supporting material section provides an insight into the *lifedesign blueprint*® for adults.

The pyramid of success holds true at any age. And the base of the pyramid starts with self-discovery and self-development as a continuum. Here's wishing all of you great success in your next search!

Value Alignment to Your Caterer and Life: The Perfect Match

The last but not the least prerequisite is the value alignment for careers and life. Values are very important in life. The values define who we are in the real light. Values have a direct impact on your career success. Knowing and communicating your personal and professional values allow you to go through life more confidently and lead to higher job satisfaction.

Attention to your values also helps to:
- Become more self-aware
- Make ethical decisions
- Prioritise your tasks

A famous quote by Roy Disney is this: **'When your values are clear to you, making decisions becomes easier.'**

Your values, whether you realise it or not, play a major role in how you choose to live your life. Your beliefs, affiliations, and relationships are all reflections of your values. Your values influence the way you spend your time, your money, and your energy. Values are not inherently good or bad. They simply define what's important to you as a human being, searching for fulfilment in all areas of your life.

Values are deeply ingrained in who we are and most of us feel an incredibly powerful connection with them – so powerful, in fact, that people all over the world since the dawn of time have been willing to die for them. Ask any soldier fighting a war why he or she is willing to risk life and limb, and the response you receive will likely be a testament to the power of values.

Values provide motivation and inspiration. They drive us to act, think, and feel. They are the fabric of who we are and how we live. It's no exaggeration to say that understanding your values is one of the most critical components of finding fulfilment in life and in your career.

Values are naturally a part of your daily thoughts, feelings, and actions. However, we often have a hard time identifying our own. An easy trick is to look at how a person uses his or her limited resources – time, money, and energy. The things to which they dedicate these resources are clear values. Additionally, you can look at the situations, people, or things that cause emotional reactions, whether good or bad. When motivation, inspiration, or joy is experienced, a value is in action. When conflict or frustration is felt, a value is being stepped on or dishonoured.

Another tool is to look at the high points and low points in life and determine how values played in these events. Whenever life provided you with a sense of pride or contribution, you were likely living in tune with your values. Whenever life resulted in a sense of personal disappointment, weakness or regret, you were likely out of step with your values.

Often, you can identify them simply based on your own self-knowledge. My top seven values are:
- Independence
- Loyalty
- Keeping my word
- Not wasting any resources
- Timely actions
- Inner peace
- Work hard and play hard

Often candidates will look for a job that will suit their skills but not necessarily a position that will fit in with their own value system of what is important to them and what motivates them. If you can understand your own set of values and motivators more specifically, it will greatly assist in defining your career choices more clearly and taking more ownership in life decisions.

The values are also finally derived from our brain preferences. Here is a short snapshot of the life and work values that you are likely to harbour based on your dominant preferences. Tick the boxes that you think apply to you.

What work values I am looking for in the job or work?

☐ Achievement ☐ Independence ☐ Power ☐ Recognition ☐ Fast pace ☐ Self-respect ☐ Influence ☐ Decision making ☐ Status ☐ High earning	☐ Strategies ☐ Taking risks ☐ Independence ☐ Opportunity to lead ☐ Diversity ☐ Time flexibility ☐ Challenges ☐ Spirituality ☐ Growth
☐ Balance ☐ Honesty ☐ Learning ☐ Personal safety ☐ Predictability ☐ Process based work ☐ Structured approach ☐ Timely delivery ☐ Stability ☐ Loyalty	☐ Team work ☐ Social Community ☐ Freedom of expression ☐ Service ☐ Affection ☐ Responsibility ☐ Giving to community ☐ Trust ☐ Contribution ☐ Belonging

Personal Values

☐ 1. Ambition ☐ 2. Altruism ☐ 3. Achievement ☐ 4. Accountability ☐ 5. Ethics/Fairness	☐ 1. Creativity ☐ 2. Uniqueness ☐ 3. Adaptability ☐ 4. Courage ☐ 5. Legacy
☐ 1. Integrity ☐ 2. Order ☐ 3. Service ☐ 4. Safekeeping ☐ 5. Balance	☐ 1. Inclusivity ☐ 2. Evaluation ☐ 3. Caring ☐ 4. Team work ☐ 5. Equality

Check how many of your values are aligned to the brain preference map. If you have not yet done your *Mybraindesign*® map, go to www.Mybraindesign®.org now.

The values are dynamic. Some of them are quite rigid. While some develop as we progress in life. It is important to be aware and see if our work and life are aligned with the values that we harbour. The values are largely inherent within each of us and are often hard-wired.

The Success Matrix

What *is* career success? Who *is* successful? Does being successful in a career translate to success in life? Why is success so overrated by the world? Why can't we celebrate failures instead? After all, failures lead us on the final path to success. Which type of thinkers are successful? Is there a particular type of brain design that decides success?

The *Mybraindesign*® program has built its own success matrix (Figure 38). It is important to map your status honestly.

Where on the Spectrum do You Fall? Which Category Defines Your Current Career Status?

Perceived success: You are feeling empty within, but the world considers you successful. Some high-paying professionals can feel the same way. You may be an engineer, chartered accountant, or doctor, but you are not fulfilled or satisfied. Essentially, you are clearly accomplished, but not successful in its true meaning.

Perceived failure: You are feeling great within as you are doing justice to your career but the world perceives you as a failure. Some artists who paint can feel the same.

Truly successful: I believe that if you have a mixture of feeling great and fulfilled while at the same time receiving world recognition for your passion and delivery, you are indeed truly successful.

Truly a failure: You are not comfortable in your career, and you are not able to make it happen otherwise. You also feel terrible inside.

People can perceive you as successful based on the benchmarks they set in their heads along with those normalised by society. While they may also perceive you to be a failure, it is important to determine what you are feeling within yourself. There is no test that can provide you with an honest review of your own feelings and emotions about success.

True success in a career is about feeling joyful and fulfilled. There is a huge difference between accomplishment and success. Many people are accomplished. They acquire competitive credentials, secure high-profile jobs, build sought-after careers and earn top-tier salaries and incomes.

These are several examples of the standards by which many in society define career success. But these items – degrees, job titles, desirable careers, and great pay – represent accomplishments. And the problem here is that accomplishments alone don't necessarily equate to career success.

	The Success Matrix	
Success	Tried and succeeded	Still trying
Failure	Tried and quit	Never tried

FIGURE 38. THE SUCCESS MATRIX (IMAGE REPRODUCED FROM CARDONEU.COM).

This success matrix is presented by Grant Cardone, who is a brilliant example of making it happen. It is highly reassuring when you hear him speak of rebellion thinking, persuasive thinking, knocking, and continuously persisting with hard work pay. His 10X program and book exemplify these concepts.

Where are you in the matrix with your big dream? Let's walk the talk as you read along. Be honest in mapping your own career success. You may also want to use this to map any dream project or work that you had desired to undertake.

> Think and ponder: GETTING A PROMOTION MEANS NOTHING IF YOU ARE UNHAPPY

Career success is a combination of achieving a reasonable level of financial stability while doing work you enjoy and then finding that you are also happy and fulfilled with your life and career choices as well.

If you love your job but find that it doesn't lead to financial self-sufficiency, career success is diminished, and if you get paid very well but lack joy or interest in your chosen career field, career success is diminished.

True career success requires an alignment between the two. The last bonus chapter highlights some of the examples of the contributory and successful brain signatures in the world. The examples will set all the theory in its right perspectives and to what we have been discussing all along in the book.

References

1. Blanchflower, D. & Oswald, A. (2008). Is well-being U-shaped over the life cycle? *Social Science & Medicine, 66*(8), 1733–1749.
2. Cote, J. E. & Levine, C.. (1987) A formulation of Erikson's theory of ego identity formation. *Developmental Review,* 7(4),273–325.
3. Gassner Otting, L. (2020). *Limitless: How to ignore everybody, carve your own path, and live your best life*, Ideapress Publishing.

4. Kahneman, D. (2011) *Thinking, fast and slow*, Farrar, Straus & Giroux.
5. Visit the work on www.geraldelman.com

Conclusion

Congratulations! You have now reached a new beginning. The successful career choice journey is always the new beginning to a life of contribution. You have come a long way in understanding how the brain works and how one can align the brain's thinking type to the work of the 21st century.

Generation Alpha is a generation that is privileged and will be challenged at the same time. Having a technological headwind is going to make a lot of jobs redundant and at the same time create new opportunities that have not existed in the world before this time. Careers such as virtual Sherpa, personal memory curator, personalised medicine expert, and Nanorobotic expert, are just around the corner. We, as the stakeholders of children – parents and teachers – must be prepared to integrate these choices right from the beginning of high school so that the seamless choice of a graduate program becomes child's play.

Most career inquiry begins at quite a late stage when the child is eleven or twelve years old. Well, this is too late indeed. We propose the methods to be introduced in early high school. Our research suggests that most children have a limited vocabulary to understand their career choices. The reason lies in the lack of transformative programs in the schools and at home. Information is aplenty on the internet but that is not being relayed in a usable form for kids. Most children are aware of only seven to ten careers. This is far less in number compared to the already mapped 800 careers available with our program. This allows a window of opportunity for hands-on activities making the children aware of the potential options in front of them.

The seven-step pyramid of career success is designed to integrate all the elements of career choice wisely. Self-discovery is the foundation and self-development is the continuum. We are all unique in our thinking patterns. Our thoughts determine our actions. We are all wired to perfection. We each have a unique set of seventeen different thinking or cognitive patterns. Each of the maps is built from the four basic building blocks of thinking – types 1 to 4 – derived from the functions of the relevant brain's cortex.

The four types of thinking are re-highlighted (Figure 40) for a rapid review.

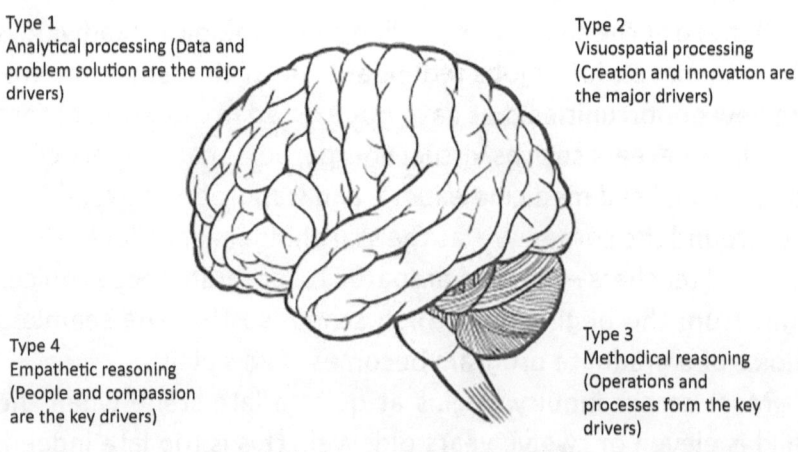

FIGURE 39. THE FOUR TYPES OF THINKING (IMAGE BY THE AUTHOR).

The career cluster maps, the indices of thinking, and the drivers all help in crafting the right career path. The interests form the central focal point around which other ways to decide the careers are placed. The *lifedesign blueprint*® encompasses the internal and external factors of career choices. All the factors that apply to choosing the right path are now aligned. These factors can stem from the availability of courses, curriculum, family support, finances, and much more. The SORT chart, outlining the strengths, opportunities, resistance and techniques to overcome the areas of resistance is mapped against the relevant brain designs to help develop the right skills. The skills that can lead the brain in its most dominant type are those that create growth while at the same time the skills in areas of resistance allow the thinking patterns to be stretched. Remember the analogy: Driving involves looking into the front mirror and the rear mirrors too for safety and precaution.

The Pyramid of Career Success Choice Holds True at Any Age

I am forty-two years old. For me, the deepest source of malaise in mid-career a few years back was not regretting the past but a sense of futility regarding the present. My work still seemed worthwhile: I saw value in treating patients, researching, and writing. Yet there was something hollow in life that loomed ahead. That is when I decided to step up and upskill by doing an MBA from Cambridge. Although daunting at the age of thirty-eight years to do a full-time rigorous and hectic program in business, it was the most fulfilling decision of my life. I could roll up my sleeves in finance, enterprise projects, writing books, coaching programs, analysing stocks, business, investing, and much more. I would have never fathomed doing this being a physician. The most important thing was an alignment between my brain's type 2 and 3 thinking patterns and the work I started to do.

The alignment brings a renewed force or energy to my everyday work. My innovative and enterprise-driven brain would not let me sleep and be satisfied with my current achievements. Achievements do not equate to success. Success is a feeling of joy and inner satisfaction which is quite subjective in nature.

Allowing the children to relate to a life-size directory of successful people and contributory brains in their respective fields who can then also teach them about their profession is our ongoing and humble endeavour. If the child relates to their career through the lens of their best thinking brain type, it allows them to understand the concept well. Our *Contributory Success Signature* program is an ongoing program that allows the successful (truly successful and not perceived) to join hands and map their brains to add their contribution to the life-size online directory.

Our brains have over 2.5 petabytes (one hundred million gigabytes) of memory, one hundred billion nerve cells to work, trillions of synapses, and a capacity to think over 50,000 thoughts. The massive untapped potential to explore and create and make magic in any career field is lying dormant in each of us. It is a matter of the right kindling. My personal vision is to ignite these normal brains to embrace this immense capacity to develop and grow. I want each child to engage in work where he or she can find his or her true self. This will create a magical nation, world, and planet. Someone rightly said, being a scientist is very fulfilling. Even if one person benefits from the research, the birth is well lived. This is my humble prayer that this work can help many a soul struggling to find their purpose and capabilities. The choice dilemma can be effectively bypassed by using this scientific methodology. The clarity for choice shall brood confidence and confidence shall bring success. I thank the great almighty and my spiritual teachers for guiding me on this path.

About the Author

Born into a family of doctors, Dr. Sweta Adatia has postgraduate degrees in medicine (Gujarat, India) and neurology (Mumbai, India). She was awarded a fellowship in Stroke Medicine and Care at the University of Calgary, Canada, is the recipient of fifteen gold medals and prizes in medicine. She also holds an MBA from the University of Cambridge, UK, specialising in finance and healthcare.

Dr. Sweta Adatia is passionate about understanding the brain and the powers of the self from the viewpoint of psychometric science and spiritual science. Along with mainstream medicine, she has completed medical courses in interventional pain care, hypnotherapy, crystal healing, basic and advanced pranic healing, clairvoyance, aura photography, and past life regression, neurofeedback, brain mapping (QEEG) and quantum healing.

Dr. Sweta Adatia's successful creation of *Mybraindesign*® endeavours to help people struggling to embrace their purpose in life in alignment with their brain's thinking preferences. She has launched *Klickcap* – a cap-way to the brain. This is a simple learning tool by which a child can learn and grow by understanding the simple concepts of the brain.

Her dream is to open a global *Future Ready* school to help younger generations prepare for their future with confidence and by empowering them to face life.

Dr. Sweta Adatia is a music lover, avid reader and global traveller. She believes in simple living and high thinking. She is a minimalist, using only thirty-one personal items as her small contribution to creating a carbon-neutral footprint. She is the founder of a charitable organisation in India helping stroke patients with the best medical care. She is also the co-founder of an organisation that makes innovative brain games. Her spiritual leanings and learnings have kept her focussed and active in achieving her goal to optimise her inner potential to benefit the world at large.

Dr. Sweta Adatia has worked in leading institutions in Asia, North America, central Africa and the Middle East, and also with the United Nations Institute for Training and Research (UNITAR).

She currently holds the position of Medical Director and Specialist Neurology at RAK Hospital in the United Arab Emirates.

Extras

Signatures of Success in the Bright Brains of the World

Our ongoing aim is to create a life-size living career success directory for children. We believe there should be enough real-life brains being showcased to children that allow them to relate to individual careers and professions. Merely being exposed to social media and relying on the information presented on the internet is not enough. It is necessary to learn about people's lives and the way their brain functions to allow them to progress with ease.

We evaluated the brain design maps for successful people in various fields. We performed a detailed quantitative electro-encephalogram (QEEG) analysis of their brains to figure out the functions of their default mode network and also analyse the firing in the areas of the executive functions and visuospatial processes.

We proceeded with the hypothesis that having a balanced brain is essential to lead. Most people who are strictly rational or limbic face the problem of also being strictly left-sided or right-sided thinkers. Having a balanced mix allows the individual to be flexible and agile in their thinking.

Let me start with my own brain design and then I will bring some fantastic profiles across whom I am sure you shall be pleased to meet.

Life-size career directory sneak peek: Watch out as more profiles are uploaded on an ongoing basis at the *Mybraindesign*® website.

Dr. Sweta Adatia

The *kindlepreneur* waking each day to kindle normal young brains into being truly successful and fulfilled by mapping their life design through her research.

Who is Dr. Sweta Adatia? By now you must know me well enough.

The *Mybraindesign*® Snapshot

Type IM, which is short for innovation ('I') and methodical ('M') reasoning: Types 2 + 3

A Deep-Dive Into the Brain

My brain profile is the classic example of a dual-combination thinking profile. Type IM or Type 2 + 3 is a combination of innovation-based processing and method-based reasoning. I am essentially attracted by innovative ideas but need to implement them to perfection. I am quite obsessed when it comes to implementation. I also have a tendency to be risky while at the same time withholding that risk.

I could not do a lot of risky things in my life because my type 3 thinking brain will just hold me back. The point to make is that having two sides of the brain that operate differently – one being methodical reasoning and the other being innovative processing – has helped me to embrace my current role as an administrator and also a passionate entrepreneur.

Well, if I would have been only a left-sided thinker, I may have been happy seeing the patients and sitting in a small office but with this brain's thinking combination, I have to act to create new cutting-edge discoveries. Thanks to knowing my brain's thinking processes, I can leverage my actions to this level.

The Brain Design to Life Design

The unique combination of thinking has helped me to wear two distinct hats in life. Without knowing my thinking pattern I could not have known if I would ever be ready to have taken risks and experiment with my own career.

The Proposed Best Supporting Brains in My Life

Any brain that exhibits a type 1 or 4 thinking orientation is going to be a great teammate and help in my life.

Moustafa Hamwi

The Brainy Introduction

The *passionpreneur* sweeping the world with undying passion as a leadership coach and founder of Passionpreneur Publishing, Australia.

Who is Moustafa?

Moustafa is an award-winning author, speaker and coach. He is considered one of the world's top experts on the use of passion to spark creativity, entice innovation and awaken the entrepreneurial spirit of a true leader. Moustafa was ranked as one of the top 100 leaders of the future (from a pool of more than 12,000 applicants) by the world's #1 Executive Coach Dr. Marshall Goldsmith, and received the nickname of 'Mr. Passion' by Prof. Tony Buzan, the inventor of mind mapping.

He has interviewed 160+ global leaders, experts, authors, coaches, award-winning artists, Nobel prize laureates and Olympians on his talk show Passion Sundays. His show has been featured on the blog of Thinkers50, the world's most prestigious ranking of the top 50 management thinkers alive.

The Career Success Spin

Moustafa started his career journey as a telesales operator after which he ran his events business. He created a multimillion-dollar events business in Dubai, UAE, but the recession swept away his investments. Stressed, in 2012 bought a one-way ticket to India. He met a swami in a cave who asked an important existential question. Realising that he has much to give the world, he headed back to Dubai to set up a series of talks and training courses to help all people, from students to chief executives, find their passion.

Mybraindesign® Snapshot

Moustafa is a combination of types 1 + 2 + 3. He thinks in three different areas of the brain almost simultaneously.

The brain's thinking type is resilient. Having a very rational brain allows him to move beyond the emotions of failure pretty quickly. He is passionate about creating magic in people's lives and uses creative and solution-driven approaches thanks to his wonderfully balanced brain.

He is continuously able to drive creative solutions through his rational thinking and to keep innovating.

The Best Supporting Brains For His Journey

His lowest preferred brain quadrant is the people-driven empathetic reasoning. This brain type can form his strength as a member of the team.

Nicole Smith-Ludvik

A professional skydiver and stunt woman who stands even taller after climbing the top of the Burj Khalifa for a viral ad shoot campaign with the Emirates airline.

Who is Nicole?

Originally from a small town in Georgia, US, Nicole is as well-rounded as she is fearless, with an impressive resume that includes a successful corporate career, professional skydiver, yoga instructor, social media influencer, stuntwoman, and all-around adventurer.

Nicole was married in her early twenties, and life took an unexpected turn when she was widowed at twenty-five. After much soul-searching, she decided to follow her passion for adventure and became a skydiver. Soon after, Nicole was involved in a car accident that killed her skydiving instructor. Nicole was critically injured, and doctors were convinced she would not survive with a broken neck, back, tailbone, a punctured lung, two broken ribs, four pelvic fractures, and two brain injuries. The rest, as they say, is history. Not only did Nicole make a full recovery, she literally went on to conquer the world, becoming one of the world's most inspirational skydivers and a stuntwoman. Nicole has been named one of the most inspirational women to look out for in 2022, holds the record for the youngest person ever to skydive in all fifty United States, and has been featured as a GoPro Creator.

With her unique life story, Nicole has drawn on her personal experiences and unexpected personal life traumas to pursue motivational speaking. She regularly speaks about overcoming fear and facing adversity and how perseverance, determination, and drive can bring success. Nicole is courageous, authentic, and inspiring to many and easily forms connections with people from all over the globe.

Mybraindesign® Snapshot

Nicole is a type 2 + 3 + 4 thinker. Her visuospatial processing with empathetic reasoning leads her thinking.

This brain profile allows people to be quite outgoing, risk-taking, imaginative, people-oriented, helpful to others, able to see the big picture, and open to ideas. This is also a profile that is supported by type 3 thinking which indicates there is always a method to the madness.

Nicole is able to pivot career roles in life easily and swiftly because of her brain type. Having only type 2 + 4 thinking could have possibly led her to vivid imagination for doing something unique but not allowing her to take effective steps. The addition of type 3 thinking allows her to filter the best of ideas and implement them. Again, this is a resilient brain type.

The Best Supporting Brains for Her Journey

Nicole does not prefer to use the quadrant that can act to subvert logical analysis and data-centric approach. Hence anyone with a type 1 thinking profile can be perfectly synergistic as a team for her.

Dr. Eng. Suaad Al Shamsi

A mother, wife, influencer and the UAE's first female aviation engineer. A pioneer who is an inspiration not just for Emirati women, but for women across the world looking to break the glass ceiling in pursuit of their passion.

Who is Dr. Suaad?

'Aviation is in my DNA,' says Suaad, who holds an honorary doctorate in her pet subject. She is the first Emirati woman to study aeronautical engineering in the UK. Suaad also did her MBA with a double major in aviation management and aeronautical engineering. She is also the DPA in aviation management and leadership at The American University in Cairo.

After her studies, and after training stints at Messier Bugatti, Honeywell, Kunz, Airbus and Boeing, Suaad flew back to the UAE to join the Emirates airline as the first female Emirati aircraft engineer in the UAE. Swiftly rising up the corporate ladder, she was put in charge of the landing gear (wheels and brakes) workshop, and was then made technical engineer and promoted to aviation maintenance during her 10-year tenure.

With more than sixteen years of experience in the industry, she is a leader *par excellence*. Currently, she is working as an aviation consultant for midfield terminal and sustainability in Abu Dhabi, UAE.

Mybraindesign® snapshot

By now you must know that a typical engineer would need only types 1 + 3 thinking. But to fully fathom what Suaad has achieved, one would have to stretch the thinking and guess her brain type?

She is indeed a type 2 + 3 contrast (Type II) thinker. Well, you have seen this type of brain earlier. I have a similar brain type. She is driven by innovation and method and tries to balance this with out-of-the-box thinking for the implementation of processes. She is likely to be full of ideas and constantly on an abstract thinking spree. She is also likely to be highly methodical in her approach at the same time. The career she has pursued is a testimony to her brain's thinking process.

Supporting brains for Dr. Suaad

Any type 1 thinker will be an asset to her team. She can be the innovative force while the other brain types can provide her with the necessary data-backed analysis.

Dr. Raza Siddiqui

Dr. Raza Siddiqui is CEO of Arabian Healthcare Group, UAE, and a driver of innovation and premium healthcare delivery in UAE.

Who is Raza Siddiqui?

Passionate, creative, innovative, and leader are some of the words that define Dr. Siddiqui. During his illustrious career spanning more than four decades, he has successfully driven many high-profile projects and bagged various awards and accolades for his pioneering work in the healthcare domain.

Starting his career as a management trainee at a young age with a leading pharmaceutical company, Lupin Laboratories, and then moving to Ranbaxy, he created a unique niche for himself in a competitive industry. After working for over a decade in that sector, he tried his hand at fashion designing for seven years, establishing his mantle once again but soon realising his true calling and passion – the healthcare sector. In 1995, he challenged himself by coordinating the successful launch of the largest corporate hospital in India, the Indraprastha Apollo Hospital. Not only did he make it financially viable in the first year of operations, producing a world record of sorts, but he also positioned it as a destination hospital for domestic as well as international medical tourists.

Realising his immense potential and contributions, the Apollo leadership entrusted him with the mission to set up the first Apollo Hospital outside India while assigning him the task of promoting India as a medical tourism destination in the Middle Eastern region. Both tasks were immaculately and successfully carried out.

Thereafter, he took up the responsibility of creating RAK Hospital, a premium healthcare facility in the UAE which quickly gained the reputation of a luxury top-notch medical tourism destination and a trusted institution for the local population.

Career Success Highlights

After completing his Bachelor of Science from Delhi University, Dr. Siddiqui began his career as a management trainee with a pharmaceutical giant in India. His thirst to learn and grow kept pushing him to pursue higher studies and that's when he embarked on a formal management degree and completed an MBA while continually climbing the corporate ladder. His immense contributions to the healthcare sector and his hunger to learn earned him three honorary doctorate degrees from esteemed universities in the USA, Europe, and the UAE.

Meeting him in 2004, Sheikh Saud Bin Saqr Al Qasimi, Member of the Supreme Council of the UAE and Ruler of Ras Al Khaimah, was quick to spot in him the visionary leader and the person who could be entrusted with the job of creating a futuristic global destination hospital. Today, RAK Hospital stands as a testament to his hard work, innovative approach, and a great example of his ingenious vision.

Dr. Siddiqui firmly says, 'You either turn your passion into your profession or be passionate about what you do and success will automatically follow.' This is the mantra he follows on a daily basis to stay focused, motivated, and always on the go. His '3Ps' of success are passion, perseverance, and positivity.

Mybraindesign® snapshot

Dr. Siddiqui is a triple thinker – a combination of types 1 + 2 + 3. He is driven by strategy and innovation while at the same time he is likely to be a fanatic data dabbler. He has a highly rational brain that can see the potential of any idea quite vividly. His rational brain can drive the choices quite appropriately by reading between the lines.

From a Bachelor of Science to marketing management in the pharmaceutical industry to a totally unrelated industry of fashion to being a CEO of a healthcare institution is testimony to his resilient and rational brain.

Supporting Brains for Dr. Siddiqui

Any thinking type 3 or 4 person who is driven by details and method with a high dosage of compassion is an ideal team member for Dr. Siddiqui.

Swamini Vimalananda

This is the most special profile of my life. I met her when I was barely sixteen years old and my life changed completely. I was taught an important lesson for realising my potential by Vedantic techniques proposed by the great guru Swami Chinmayananda.

Who is Swamini Vimalananda?

After acquiring an Honours degree in architecture, her travels made her reflect on life and move from designing the world of outer space to seeking a sacred inner space. The Chinmaya Mission Vedanta Course deepened her spiritual knowledge.

Her passion for education found fulfilment in concretising her Guru's vision into the Chinmaya Vision Programme (CVP) which now largely features in the National Education Policy (NEP) introduced in July 2020 by India's Central Government. Her multifarious contribution in the field of education as she headed the Chinmaya Mission Educational Cell for 25 years has touched the lives of millions.

A dynamic leader, a serious seeker, a spiritual practitioner, a prodigious learner, a visionary educator, a nature lover, a prolific writer and a popular speaker, she travels around the world guiding seekers of all age groups. Her simple style of talking has captivated the intellectual and faithful alike. Her sense of aesthetics and depth of knowledge reflects in all her activities, including her writing.

Career Success Highlights

Swamini has always been curious about life. Just as she was about to begin an illustrious career as an architect at a top school, she decided to embrace life as a monk. She has worked for over 30 years in the field of education. She has authored books on a variety of subjects including Vedantic commentaries, Indian culture series, answering youth queries, child-centred activities and education theories. Her books are very popular as are her YouTube talks (@Best of Swamini Vimalananda).

Mybraindesign® snapshot

Swamini is a very powerful type 2 thinker. Innovative ideas flow to her like a rain shower. She is quite instrumental in creating multiple programs for the youth schools and as head of the Chinmaya education cell. She currently spends nine months in silence and the remaining three months preaching the Vedantic Indian traditional texts.

Her supporting brains

She exclaims of always being supported by type 1 + 3 thinkers in her life. And all of the innovative approaches that she visualises, her team manifests.

Want More Resources?

Are you Future Ready? Please visit our website www.schooloffutures.com OR www.mybraindesign.org for more details.

Mybraindesign® Individual Package

Get insights about your thinking types and pattern through the *Mybraindesign*® map.
    Explore your innate strengths and opportunities.
    Explore the *Lifedesign blueprint*® & SORT charts for you

Pyramid of Career Success Bundle for High School Students

Mybraindesign® assessment code with personal counselling about the best career choice.
    Explore the Career Quest workbooks available in junior and senior versions
    Finalize the choice of career confidently and successfully

Mylifedesign Plug and Play for schools

Adopt the career program in your school in the shortest time frame
- Start counselling the smart way for high schoolers
- Bundled offerings available with profit-sharing

5 Minute Career Choice Magic

A *five-minute per career masterclass* is available at https://Mybraindesign®.thinkific.com/ Enrol today to gain insights about most career courses in just sixty minutes.

More About Me and Our Work can also be found on www.drswetaadatia.com

Please visit us on https://www.schooloffutures.com/ for our programs for high school students

Mybraindesign® Speaks

We regularly offer seminars for career and life design. We conduct two *lifedesign* seminars a year. The timetable can be accessed on our website. I would also be happy to engage and deliver individual talks and seminars based on the requests.

To request a *Mybraindesign®* talk please fill out the form and get back to me at https://forms.gle/LHm5FxVKFkJZbuGB7 or scan the QR below.

Career Success Life-size Directory

We welcome successful people in various fields of IT, healthcare, the arts, creative design, influencer, AI/ML builders and any career which we missed throughout the book to work with us and showcase your best brain design as an inspiration moment for Generation Alpha.

You are the star in their lives. We will make you shine in our galaxy. Click to connect with us on our website.

About the Book

'The two most important days in your life are the day you are born and the day you find out why you are born.'

— MARK TWAIN

Your *brain design* determines your *life design*. The way you think determines the way you behave, communicate, develop relationships, advance your career, and even raise kids. Hacking this thinking is a masterful science and art. Dr. Sweta Adatia believes that being successful and not merely accomplished means cracking the human code from the inside out.

This book showcases the science of self-discovery which leads to self-development as a continuum. The author narrates the pyramid of career choice success (a seven-level process), which has been applied to thousands of students globally, applying cutting-edge neuroscience principles to the science of career choice.

This is a book for young and old. It is for the young post-college student seeking insights on the newest degrees or a parent seeking help for their young child confused about opting for the best career choice following high school. It is also for school counsellors willing to go the extra mile to help students succeed in picking the right career choice.

The 21st-century world of work is going to be different. Knowing the digital/robotic trends and staying updated about the newest career choices is no longer a luxury. It is a basic need. This book provides the tools through which children can learn more than 800 careers in a few days. The idea is to 'expose them young'. Starting early and starting right means getting half the job done for future career choices.

Dr. Sweta is intrigued about the 'X factor' that determines career success for a few people in any industry. She has collaborated with scientists in Singapore and the USA and has ongoing research – ABC of success (anatomy, biology and cognitive science of success). She is highly passionate about mapping the brain design of children and matching it to their EEG rhythms (the firing of the brain cells captured through an instrument).

Her message throughout the book is straightforward – scientific management of life's career choices is an antidote to wishful thinking for career success. Each child has the potential to achieve a great career. And it all starts with an insight into their brain make-up.

Testimonials

"I have journeyed with Dr Sweta Adatia for the last 22 years and have seen her grow from a brilliant student to a brilliant, hard-working and passionate professional as well as a selfless and compassionate human being. Her intellectual and emotional blossoming is enhanced by her spiritual seeking. An understanding of how our brain works makes us efficient and smart. Dr Sweta did my brain-mapping 12 years ago. That helped me in managing myself, and guiding people, institutions and projects. Also, career choice is a major decision which needs expert help. I believe Dr Sweta's science-based, user-friendly book will prove a great help to parents, teachers and their wards in making the right career and life choices so they can also be future ready."

—Swamini Vimalananda
Monk, Author & Past Lead of Chinmaya
Vision Program (heading over 52 schools and 7 colleges),
Chinmaya Mission Worldwide, India.

"Dr Sweta Adatia is a dear friend and a colleague from Cambridge Judge Business school. Being an orthopedic surgeon and a medic myself, I am always curious to learn about behaviours. Predictability, communication within teams helps in any profession and personal relations. I underwent the Mybraindesign assessment myself and am clearly a type 4 thinker – I love people! That's why I went into medicine. I also learned some things I need to work on and areas where I need to grow my skills. Knowing how to push the limits for oneself is such an important path to success. I am sure the parents and teachers reading this will find it a goldmine of self-exploration and growth for their children and themselves."

—Dr Taylor D Otteson
Orthopedic Surgeon Resident at Harvard, USA
& Founder of KVM and Global Scalpels Podcast

"Choosing a career in the 21st century is daunting. It is an anxiety-riddled process. My wife and I were not sure what we should choose for our daughter who is a math wizard but at the same time loves designing. We used to often question her behaviour and never understood that it was stemming from the way her thinking was designed. We never understood the functions of the brain – rational or emotional – until we explored the assessment Mybraindesign. We were totally new to the assessment. Frankly, I was quite sceptical in the beginning. But doing the assessment and seeing almost a picture-perfect report made me fall in love with the process. I advise any parent looking for advice regarding the future of his or her kid to go through the process. I totally recommend this book."

—Jack O'Neal
Serial Entrepreneur and proud father of Remy O'Neal, USA

"I wanted some data for basing my decision about the masters program. I was already pursuing a bachelors degree. I was surprised at the accuracy of my personality and behaviour traits stemming from the report. I was amazed at the number of options that opened up in front of me just by knowing my brain type. I have done many psychometric tests in the past and I thought this would be one such test, but this was not a psychometric analysis. It was an in-depth review of my thinking patterns. It was easy to do and the report was also easy to understand. I would recommend the assessment and the book which further elaborates the method to anyone from high school to adult who wants to make a firm career choice decision."

—Alark Thakkar
India, Post graduate student pursuing business

"Dr. Sweta Adatia helped Neeraj (my son) understand his strengths and interests while broadening his perspectives on the options he had. The assessment gave in-depth insights on strengths and opportunities for him. Dr. Sweta helped Neeraj discover his passion and compatibility for data science and economics. She had a very easy yet methodical approach to counselling as she incorporated and considered many factors such as cultural environment, types of courses and the future job market. I am sure this book would be very useful for all the parents and teachers concerned about the futures of their children. The 21st century choices are wide and confusing. Drawing a choice from over 800 careers can become child's play through this book and Mybraindesign."

—Cherag Shah
Head of Company Control Unit Ericason Dubai, Middle East

"Generation Alpha must wade through oceans of information, hoping they might discover their perfect career destiny. Through unveiling her Ikigai and life-calling, Sweta Adatia provides neuroscience-based research and practical tools, easing their perilous journey towards a joyous career with purpose and fulfilment.

Sweta reminds us again how to tap into the liberation of potential dreaming, to build altars of gratitude and confirms that the story we think about ourselves and our career, will determine its outcomes."

—Anna Dos Santos (MA. RPC. MPCC-S. RMFT-S.)
Counselling, Art Therapy, Marriage and Family Therapy, Critical Incidents, Clinical Supervision, Life & Career Strategist

Notes

www.ingramcontent.com/pod-product-compliance
Lightning Source LLC
Chambersburg PA
CBHW030035100526
44590CB00011B/211